Thriving Through Transition

Self-Care for Parents of Transgender Children

Denise O'Doherty

Table of Contents

Introduction
Why Focus on the Parent?

Confused. Shocked. Resentful. Angry. Lonely.
Overwhelmed. Doubtful. Powerless. Frustrated.
Sad. Hurt. Bitter. Uncomfortable. Sorrowful.
Anxious. Stunned. Perplexed. Afraid. Disturbed.
Surprised. Ashamed. Unclear. Indignant. Helpless.
Disgusted. Exasperated. Concerned. Bewildered.
Irritated. Mortified. Worried. Apprehensive.
Disappointed. Anguished. Paralyzed. Mournful.
Apologetic. Distressed. Relieved. If your child has
come out as transgender, chances are you've felt at
least one of these emotions. It's possible that you've
felt many. You're not alone.

According to the New York Times article "Raising a
Transgender Child" written by Rachel Rabkin
Peachman and published on January 31, 2017, 1.4
million adults in the United States identify themselves
as transgender. These adults were once children with
parents or caretakers who may have had little or no
knowledge of what it means to raise a transgender
child and how to take care of themselves while doing
so. Parents are confused when they find out their
child is transgender and may feel even more
confused when they hear that their child wants to

live as the other sex. Whether raising a young child, or hearing this from an adult child, many parents are shocked and don't know what to do. Parents who felt grounded and secure with their role as a parent often report feeling stunned and overwhelmed, as if they are experiencing a surreal situation. And now, without their consent, they are brought into a situation where they may be asked to make profound changes in their relationship with their child and with their behavior towards their child. Often parents feel these changes are unexpected, unwanted and undeserved. Some parents resent hearing their child wants to make changes. They may feel they do not have the ability to support their child through these changes. They may doubt themselves as parents and question, "How can I support my child when I'm not even aware of the changes that are about to happen?" Parents who were once grounded in their role as parents, may now question their ability to see their child in a different gender and question their ability to relate and parent appropriately. Parents may also feel powerless and confused about the future and what it will bring.

As a result of being told their child is transgender, parents are often caught off guard, faced to deal with something completely unexpected and left wondering where to go from here. A child's transition can affect a parent's relationship with others: siblings, friends, spouse's family, co-workers, acquaintances, etc. It may also affect their role in the family and how they see their future. Therefore, it is essential that parents get the understanding and support they need, to ease the shock, not feel so alone and have some idea of how to move forward. That means knowing how to take care of their own needs and knowing how to raise a transgender child. How parents do it, affects the quality of their own lives, their child's life, the family, the community they live in and the world.

When one person in the family transitions, the rest of the family is in transition as well, because roles and expectations change for everyone. Therefore, transition provides uncomfortable and unfamiliar situations. Parents find themselves adjusting to a relationship that looks and feels different from what is familiar. They are faced with a multitude of non-mainstream issues pushing them beyond their comfort zone. Yet, transition can also provide wonderful opportunities to gain strength and wisdom. It provides opportunities for personal growth and spiritual breakthroughs. It can foster tremendous empathy, compassion and creativity. It can deepen the meaning of love and parenting. By understanding the dynamics of the transition process, parents can learn how to minimize pain and facilitate new levels of awareness and a deeper relationship with their child, themselves and others.

This book was written to help parents make necessary adjustments to thrive through both their child's and their own transition. It helps parents face their fears, overcome resistance and know how to take care of themselves in the process. It was written to make the journey easier for parents. It is a result of my findings from working with parents of transgender children for more than two decades. In addition to parents, it was written for other family members, teachers, educators, clergy, counselors, therapists, psychologists, psychiatrists, nurses, other related health care professionals and anyone who loves a transgender person, to educate and emphasize the importance of love and compassion deserving of transgender children and to the parents who raise them.

I have seen parents go from anguish to a loving acceptance. Using the tools, insights and ideas in this book, parents can enhance and increase their education, compassion, patience, personal growth and coping skills while dealing with their child's transition. They can also continue to love themselves, their child and their role as a parent. They can heal, go forward and thrive.

Notes from the Author

I want to clarify that when talking about "your child" this can mean a young child, (elementary or middle school age), a teenager (high school), a young adult, middle age adult or older adult. The suggestions given in the book are to be taken according to the child's ability to understand and respond. When suggested that you ask your child to tell you what "coming out" has meant to them, it is obvious that this would not be appropriate for a five-year-old but would for an older child. And, you would not have to talk to teachers for a 55-year-old. Therefore, take the suggestions given and apply them to match the appropriate age of the child, keeping in mind that all who transition need support, kindness and compassion no matter what the age or situation. Also, the author acknowledges that all children are not raised by parents. Some are raised by extended family members, friends of parents, caretakers or others who had the role of raising children. Although this book refers to "parents," it honors all caregivers respectfully.

Most importantly, I realize that all parents of transgender children are not distraught. When a child makes an announcement, or the parent comes to the realization that their child is transgender, some parents feel relieved and often happy! Some parents are relieved because they now have an answer to signs they were seeing. It may explain some of the behaviors and choices they were noticing from their child. If they have seen their child struggle, they may be happy they have now come to realize what it was all about. Even if there were no signs, many parents want to see their child live authentically and fully "as they truly are." Many parents embrace their children as transgender. Many are in full support of their child coming out and many are in full support of transition. Some parents are open to accept what changes this will bring and excited about going on this journey with them. Not all parents, caregivers and family members struggle. This book is for parents and those who do.

Chapter 1
Shock

I n one second our lives can change forever. And this is what happens to some parents when a child announces to them, that he/she is transgender. Immediately, parents are surprised, and often shocked. Your body feels emotionally charged. You no longer feel at ease. You may wonder what transgender means. You sense that this news is going to change your world, and it will. But how? We have all felt the surprise and sometimes the disappointment of having an expectation that doesn't get met. When you had your child, you may have thought, at least in terms of gender, what you could expect. If you had a boy, you expected he would grow to be a man. If you had a girl, you expected she would grow to be a woman. You also expected that your child would do the things expected of a man or woman according to society's norms. Maybe all you ever wanted was to be a mother or father especially to a girl or boy. But now you are getting a sense that gender is not as simple as you thought…at least not with your child. Your emotions are now on a roller coaster ride.

Whether a parent had a suspicion that "something was different," or even if they had no idea, they

1

often report shock and disbelief as their first reactions. Parents are dealing with the idea that their life, their relationship to their child, and their role as a parent, are going to be altered. Initially, they may have little idea as to what will happen or what it will look like. Often parents are feeling betrayed that the role they valued, nurtured and cherished as a parent is now changing forever and without their consent.

Parents have many different reactions. Some parents love their child but are furiously angry at the same time. Some parents understood gender issues and transition before their child told them. This doesn't necessarily make it easier. Some want to learn what struggles their child has had regarding their gender. Some want to understand and support their child and make any changes necessary to help their child feel complete. Some are sad realizing how terrified their child was by having to muster the courage to come out to them. They are sad to know that their child, especially if they are adult, had lived so much of his/her childhood and young adult life in confusion, fear, frustration, loneliness and pain. Some parents are doubtful, particularly if this isn't the first-time new identities have been tried. Parents are also frustrated if their child came out as non-binary or gender neutral and requested that they be addressed as "them," or by a new name. Many factors influence the way a parent will respond and deal with their child coming out as transgender and making a transition. Some parents struggle a lot and some very little. Some feel grief immediately, for a multitude of reasons, but particularly if they are comfortable with their relationship as it is. Almost all parents are fearful for their child's safety and social acceptance.

A difficult issue many parents find shocking is when they hear their child wants to live as the opposite sex when it appeared to them, they were happy in the gender they were raised. When a person's physical sex does not match their gender identity they can have tremendous anxiety, pain and anguish. This is known as gender dysphoria. Transitioning to the correct gender, can alleviate gender dysphoria.

Some children display symptoms of frustration about their gender early in life. Others may not. Some children don't give any indication they have gender dysphoria growing up. They may appear comfortable in the gender with which they have been raised. Therefore, some parents are shocked and in disbelief when their child comes out to them as transgender years later. These children may have felt different from their peers growing up but didn't know why. They may have hidden their feelings out of fear of rejection. Just because a child tells you they discovered later in life that they are transgender, doesn't mean they are less transgender than a child who has symptoms in early childhood. It's not the length of time that one knows that matters, it's the depth of the feeling of discomfort of living in the wrong gender that matters.

Finding Out

Hearing your child is transgender can be the last thing most parents expect to hear. Sometimes the way you find out adds to the shock and denial. Were you told directly from your child? Does that matter to you? You may be disappointed your child didn't come to you first. Some parents find out on Facebook, looking through their child's phone texts, from another family member or from a family friend. Parents find out anywhere and everywhere. If the way you found out was not the way you would have liked, it may be a contributing factor to your initial reaction.

Bruce
Bruce began displaying effeminate characteristics when he was in high school. He told his parents he was gay when he was 15. Both parents were accepting and supportive. Recently, Bruce graduated from college and moved back home. Within the first two weeks, Bruce had

some friends over, and Linda, his mother, heard his friends refer to Bruce as "Brenda." She confronted him after they left, and he said he was planning to make a transition from male to female, and that Brenda was his chosen and preferred name. Linda felt betrayed that he didn't tell her on his own and because he had told his friends before her. She felt she was a consistent and loving mother throughout his life and felt particularly rejected and hurt that he didn't trust her to be as accepting as she had been when he told her he was gay.

Bobby

Bobby's dad noticed that his 16-year-old son was an avid reader of magazines that catered to women. i.e. Cosmopolitan, Vanity Fair, etc. He then noticed a stack of Sports Illustrated Swimsuit Editions. He was relieved, thinking his son was having a sexual interest in the women in Sports Illustrated. He decided to confront him on his stack of magazines and said to him, "I used to like thinking about being with the girls in those pictures too". His son replied, "No dad, I don't want to have them, I want to be them." Bobby's dad wondered why his son didn't talk with him about his feelings sooner.

Tanya

Tanya was an upstanding parishioner at her church where she volunteered as an usher for 20 years. She and her two sons were well known there. Both sons were married and had children. Recently, her oldest son confided to her that he was getting a divorce. He made it clear that he wasn't telling anyone else until after he and his wife decided how they were going to tell their children. He also said he would give her more details in time. Although sad, Tanya continued to talk with him and attend church. The last Sunday she attended, two of the other ushers commented to her how sorry they were to hear that her son was getting a divorce. They also said how sorry they were to hear the reason why. Tanya was shocked to learn that others knew her son was getting divorced and extremely embarrassed since they appeared to know the reason why and she didn't. It appears that her son's angry wife had announced to most of the congregation that she was getting a divorce because her husband was transgender.

Many parents are told after the fact. They may be told when their children are beginning hormones, after they have started hormones or even before or after they are having surgery. They may have found out via Facebook, other social media or through another family member or friend. There may be many reasons why the child waited. Some parents find out that their child is attending a transgender support group or other LGBT support group and wonder why, only to find out later. If you are angry, try and talk it over with your child calmly, and discuss it. You may find out their fears regarding telling you were not necessarily about you. If it is about you, ask what you can do to be included in the future. *They may have waited to tell you because they were dealing with their own struggle with self-acceptance.* Letting them know how you feel may reinforce how important they are to you and that you want to be important to them.

Many adult children come out via letter, particularly if they don't live close. This gives the advantage of allowing parents time to digest and adjust to the news. Often the parent's initial reaction is not the true reaction. Often the adult child does not want to be there for the initial response but wants to see the parents after they have had time to think and process.

For other parents, finding out is not much of a surprise. They may have seen their child displaying signs and symptoms uncharacteristic of their birth sex. Some may have thought their child was lesbian or gay. Parents often suspect sexuality before gender.

Parent Emotions / Questions / Reactions at this Stage

Parents often say or feel the following:

"I knew something was different but thought they would grow out of it."

Some parents know something is different with their child from an early age. They might think depending on their age, that the child "will grow out of it." It is not uncommon to see young girls and boys prior to puberty play with toys, dress in outfits, or participate in stereotypical games and activities associated with the opposite sex. At puberty, most children take on the stereotypic norms of their biological sex and move on developmentally. Transgender children, on the other hand, often do not. They continue to be attracted to the things associated with the gender to which they relate. Transgender kids often dislike puberty because it is a reminder that they are in a body that does not match their vision of themselves as their true gender.

Children come out at all ages, even up to late adulthood. Most people who think they might be transgender, explore and research all they can, often months or even years prior to coming out. Finding resources, information and facts about gender can be helpful and supportive when looking to identify their feelings and validate their true gender identity.

Prior to coming out, many children with gender dysphoria wait to tell their parents because they are worried about their reaction, worried they will get upset, worried that they will guilt them about it, or worried that they might want to try and change their mind. They may be fearful that it will change their relationship with their parent and of course, worried that the parent won't love them anymore. Even when children are close to their parents, the parents are sometimes the last to know. It is too hard for some children to imagine a downward change in their relationship with their parent, or worse, that they will be abandoned. Some teens may wait because they feel they can't do anything to make a change without their parent's approval since they are both emotionally and financially dependent and fearful the parent will cut them off.

"If only he was gay." / "If only she were lesbian."

Many parents go to the "If only" they were gay or lesbian, thinking they could handle this better if that were the case. This is probably because it is more socially accepted and because they feel it would be safer and easier for their child. Comparisons and "what if's" don't help.

Being lesbian or gay refers to someone who is sexually attracted to the same sex. This is independent of gender. Being transgender is when someone's gender identity (the way they see themselves) does not match the genitalia they were given at birth. Some people may go through a period, where they think they are lesbian or gay before they are aware they are transgender.

Many people know their sexual orientation sooner than their gender orientation. Sometimes gender orientation comes early, sometimes later. Some people with gender dysphoria, know they don't relate to the gender they were given at birth, but they don't know there are alternatives to feeling stuck and imprisoned. Some people are not aware they can be free from a life of misery and pretense.

Some people stay hidden to avoid rejection from their parents, their religion, their culture, etc. People of all ages often report in therapy that prior to coming out as transgender, they didn't think there were any viable options.

"How could I have not seen this coming?"

You didn't see it because you weren't looking. Sometimes there are signs and sometimes there aren't. Transgender children of all ages, whether they are young, teenagers, young adults or adults need time to process their feelings about themselves. Most exploration is hidden until they are sure. Blaming yourself won't change anything. The focus needs to be on where to go from here.

"How could he/she do this to me?"

Your child is not doing this to you. He/she is on their own path with their own life. Figuring out one's gender is not as easy for some as others. Although it may feel extremely personal, it is not a personal attack on you.

"How am I supposed to live in world where my son/ daughter doesn't exist anymore?"

Adjusting to this change for some is the hardest of all- at first. Grieving this will take time and patience. You will replace your grief in time with other fine and wonderful things to do and experience with your child. Your relationship will continue to grow with love and understanding, if you let it. He or she is still the child you raised and nurtured. He or she is still your child to love.

"How am I supposed to handle people who try and comfort me but have no idea what I'm going through?"

Be patient. No, they may not have a clue. But, go with their good intentions and try and be kind. Stay surrounded with those who **do** "get it." Those who know exactly what you are going through and who will be there for you. Check in with them regularly, not just when you need to talk. This will keep you feeling supported and balanced and give you something to look forward to.

"I'm tired of telling people I'm fine."

You may not be fine. So, pull back if you need to. Do what it takes to function. Take care of yourself. Know that not being fine is temporary and you will feel better and more like yourself with time.

"What did I do so wrong that this should be happening to me?"

Nothing. Blaming is not the answer. Don't compare. This is not your fault, nor is it your spouse's fault, your ex's, the transgender community, God, no one. This is the way it is for your child. Corrections can be made so they can have a life where they can express themselves and be treated as the gender they are.

"Is God punishing me?"

"I find the whole concept of a loving god to be very disappointing at this point", said one middle aged mother with a transgender daughter. Working though religious beliefs is very individual. Faith can help us meet challenges. Find support where you worship if you feel it will help you. But remember, this is no punishment. Challenges happen to everyone. Everyone has problems. Blame does not get us anywhere. We are all brought into this world to find meaning and purpose. That includes you and your child. We are all here on our own path to find our own way.

"I just want more time with him/ her in the gender they look like now."

This is perfectly understandable. You are used to raising a child of a particular gender. You didn't think that would change. You love them for who you know them to be and a change seems foreign and unfamiliar. No one wants to let go of someone or something they love. Feeling this loss is grief. It can be helpful to remember you still have your child to love and who needs you.

Denise O'Doherty

"I'm angry at my spouse for not being there for me."

It can be harder to deal with this if you and your spouse are not equally supportive of your child. You don't have to feel the same, but it would be helpful to agree to disagree, and respect your differences. Disapproving parents often change with time, particularly when they learn more about gender and when they see their child happier. Letting your differences put stress on your relationship can make it more difficult.

Feeling betrayed by older children.

Some parents are informed by their older children that they are about to transition, without having shared any history of their dysphoria with their parents. Parents often feel hurt and angry that they were not told more or that they were not a part of the process. This may be particularly hard if you thought you had a close relationship with your child. You may now feel your child does not value you or your opinion. Being the last to know, or not the first, makes some parents feel left out and unimportant.

All these feelings, and many others that you may be feeling, are understandable. You are not alone. You may feel overwhelmed and as if you are on a roller

14

coaster. Be patient with yourself and the situation. This is the beginning of a process that will make more sense with time. For now, try and be patient with yourself and the process.

13 Reasons Why It's Difficult for Parents

1) **Parents often feel they have no one to talk to about something so personal.**

Parents often feel their situation is so unique, that no one will understand and therefore they will have to deal with it alone. Some parents won't speak to anyone because they have shame and feel responsible for their child's feelings. Some parents don't want to "burden" others with a problem that is not theirs. Or worse, they fear getting sympathy or pity. They may also fear another parent might smugly walk away thinking "I'm glad I don't have that problem." A parent might fear that others may judge or criticize their child out of their own ignorance, fear or lack of compassion. You spend a life time raising your child to fit in and now they are telling you they don't. A parent may wonder how they can expect support from others, even close friends and family, when they themselves are experiencing doubts and concerns.

2) **Learning a new language – Gender and Gender Terms**

When a person changes outwardly from one gender to another and lives in accordance with their gender identity, it is called going through transition, or transitioning. Transition can occur in two ways: 1) social transition through non-permanent changes, for example with clothing, hairstyle, name change, using different pronouns and 2) medical transition using medicines and/or surgeries to promote gender-based body changes.

<u>Bob</u>
Bob, an accountant, grew up always feeling he had to hide his "feminine" side, a feeling that increased as he grew older. At 55, he decided to transition and live full time as a female. Bob did not choose to have surgery, but he did take hormones and made outward changes to dress and present as a female full-time. Because of the hormones, we would say Bob has made a medical transition.

<u>Margaret</u>
Margaret has a 13-year-old child who was born male but who has been presenting as female since "he" was 8 years old. Although their child was named Nathan at birth, Nathan has been dressing as a girl and has chosen the name "Nancy." Margaret has gone to Nancy's high school where the teachers and principal are very

supportive. They changed rosters and forms at school, so Nancy would be called her preferred name and be treated as a girl. Nancy does not take hormones and has had no surgery but looks and acts like a female. Her identity and gender expression are both female. Everyone who meets Nancy, thinks she is a genetic girl. Nancy has made a social transition.

Terms like transgender, gender dysphoria, gender variant, gender identity, gender queer, and gender expression may be unfamiliar. Parents don't think of gender dysphoria as being a common issue when raising kids. For most people, their gender matches their sex. In other words, our thinking about who we are in terms of being feminine or masculine, matches the genitals that we were given at birth. You may have been taught that if you were born with a penis, you are a boy and would think "the way a boy thinks" given his society and culture. If you were born with a vagina, you would think you were a girl and would "think like a girl" according to the norms in society. Today we know that although this is true for some, it certainly is not true for everyone. Gender is fluid, meaning that men and women have a far greater capacity to feel and express their gender (male or female identity) with a comfort level that exceeds their genitals and the limited gender norms of our binary society. Some people, therefore consider themselves to be non-binary or gender non-conforming, and don't conform to conventional male or female stereotype expression or behavior.

Karla
Karla, a 63-year-old high school principal, came to therapy after her 43-year-old daughter Marilyn, announced to her parents that she feels she has gender dysphoria and is non-binary, meaning she doesn't see herself as male or female. She made a request that from now on, Karla and her husband refer to her as "Mica" since it sounded more androgynous, and coordinate it with pronouns such as "they, them" instead of "she or her." Karla knew her daughter was never a "girly -girl" but was stunned having never heard of anything like this before.

Many mentally healthy people live outside the "box" of what our society says is masculine or feminine. Gender dysphoria can be present when a person is in distress because their gender identity (how they mentally perceive themselves as male or female) does not match their genitals at birth. (Your genitals at birth are your sex) In other words when a "male-bodied" person, does not feel, think, or have a perception that either all or part of himself is a male, and is disturbed by this, he has gender dysphoria. When a "female bodied" person does not feel, think or have a perception that either all or part of herself is female and is disturbed by this, she has gender dysphoria. Genitals do not determine how all people think of themselves in terms of gender identity.

Many people have various expressions of male and female. Not everyone fits into a box. Many people are intersex, which means that they are born with any of several variations of sex hormones or genitals that do not fit typical definitions of male or female. Being intersex or having gender dysphoria are conditions. Some people with a great amount of gender dysphoria make a transition, to correct their dysphoria. That way they can feel comfortable having a body that matches their mental perception of who they are. They can have the peace of mind to live in a world where people see and treat them as they are. Imagine the misery of living in a body every day where people have expectations of you to be a gender that you are not. Imagine growing up feeling you are male and being expected to dress, act and identify as female. The pain may be so great that many people who are misunderstood about this become suicidal. Imagine being a teenage boy who dreams of being female, marrying a man, having a family, being a mother and being active in women's organizations. Yet, when he tells anyone, they discount, ignore and divert his feelings with a response like, "you are probably gay." Most people have little personal experience to understand the severe physical, emotional, spiritual and sexual discomfort one experiences when they live in a world where people perceive them as someone they are not. When you think in one gender but live in the body of another one is limited as to how active and involved they can participate in life. Where every minute of every day with every decision you make, you force yourself to think or act unauthentically, because if you acted the way you really felt, you would be shamed.

Many people have gender dysphoria. There are different degrees of it and different manifestations of it. Not all people with gender dysphoria transition. Some enjoy the fact that they are outside a main-stream model and they appreciate the wider spectrum in which they see themselves. Some may not feel their symptoms are problematic enough to make a transition. They may be comfortable with their gender being non-main stream and appreciate that part of themselves. When it comes to your own child, you may want to find out what degree of discomfort your child experiences presently and what degree of discomfort they have had in the past.

Understanding your child's gender identity and expression can be bonding and educational. If they are old enough to speak with you about this, an open and honest talk can be a great way for you to get to know where he/she is on the gender spectrum. It can help you know more about where they are in their life. Gender terms are specifically defined in the glossary in the back of this book.

Loss of your role as parent to a male/female

Some people know when they have a child that they prefer either a boy instead of a girl, or a girl instead of a boy. Some people have no preference and just want a healthy baby with "10 fingers and 10 toes." It can be particularly difficult for a parent who longed for a girl, to have to let go of her daughter, when a female child is what she longed for. The same can be true of a parent who longed for a male child.

As a parent, you probably spent years literally teaching this special human being, your child, how to be a boy or girl. Ironically, depending on the age of the child, you may be teaching them how to be the other gender. If your child comes out later in life, your adjustment is about accepting their change and changing the way you relate to them.

It's particularly hard when parents mourn the loss of the external image and the significance attached to the way they relate to that image. "My sweet little girl", "my son the doctor", "my son the soldier", "my daughter, the soprano singer." Having had these perceptions may make it harder to adapt to the child's new identity role.

It can be more confusing if you watched your child enjoy their life in the gender that matches their sex for all or most of their lives. Maybe she did enjoy ballet, or he did enjoy being an Eagle Scout. Some people appreciate their life prior to transition and some don't. If they dreaded each day having to participate in activities they didn't like and be identified as someone they weren't, the past can feel like pain. Others cherish certain events and memories in the past and are grateful for how these events have influenced them to be the people they are today. Either way, for the parent, the past is still valid. You can keep your wonderful memories and all you did for them. You can cherish those times that you hold dearly and know that this doesn't have to make that go away for you. Whether they enjoyed the events of the past or not, it doesn't mean they don't appreciate you and all you did for them. It just means they want to be loved and accepted by you, for who they are now.

Many parents love the bond they have with their child and love the relationship they have together as it is now. They love their child and the bond they have had with their child since birth. It can be very difficult thinking that this bond can change permanently. It can be hard for parents to see themselves adjusting to seeing their child in a different gender. The meaning one gives to their child's gender may be a factor in how difficult dealing with changes will be.

<u>William</u>
A 55-year-old businessman came to see me for therapy. He cordially shook my hand and smiled. He sat down slowly and looked me straight in the eyes. Then he leaned forward, with both elbows on his lap, put his face in his hands and proceeded to weep. He wept for 15 minutes straight, unable to bring himself to speak. Then, he looked up at me, and said, "I don't have a son anymore," and he proceeded to weep some more. Later that session, I found out that he was divorced, and this son was his only child. They enjoyed doing many activities together for many years. He taught his son baseball and hockey. They went hunting and fishing. They attended various sports together and his son appeared to be his best friend and his pride and joy. He loved his son dearly. He loved his role as a father and he loved thinking about the things they would do together in the future. He was an only child himself. His child's need to transition changed his world since his son was the most important person in his life and he loved the life they had together. He couldn't perceive what his life would be like without him. He

*couldn't imagine their relationship not being able to
continue. Seeing it any other way at this point, was not
something he had ever considered. He was not able to
imagine having a daughter. His grief was overwhelming.
He couldn't perceive his identity or his life without
his son.*

3) **Accepting your child's changing appearance and Identity.**

Parents often have a deep sense of loss when they
discover their child will be changing in outward
appearance and identity. Many parents have years of
memories seeing their child acting, dressing,
speaking, playing, making friends and growing up
in the gender connected to their sex at birth. If you
watched your daughter grow up as a little girl, no
doubt you have had thoughts of her growing up as a
girl and continuing this for life. Maybe you envisioned
a wedding, engagement, being a grandparent to her
children. It is understandable to have had these
visions. It is the same for boys. There may be
stereotyped activities you had hoped to share with
them. Now your son, is shaving his legs, letting his
hair grow out and wearing nail polish. Your daughter
wants her breasts removed and is talking about
having facial hair, starting testosterone so her voice
will change, and becoming masculine. You may
have given your child a name at birth that had

special meaning to you. Now you may be watching them find joy in replacing it so easily, with another that has no meaning to you. Seeing your child ecstatic with their upcoming changes when you are dealing with loss and resistance is difficult.

One parent came to therapy saying, "I walked in on my 16-year-old daughter last week when she was changing from her gym clothes to jeans and a tee shirt. I noticed she was binding her breasts with a tight tank top and a sports bra over it. I thought she had just been a "late bloomer" and hadn't developed yet. When I asked what was going on, she said she had been binding her breasts for 2 years. Then she announced, "When I turn 18-year-old, I will be taking testosterone and making changes to my body, so I can be a boy. I am a boy."

<u>Thomas</u>
Thomas came to therapy having difficulty accepting his 22-year-old son's transition. Even though his son had been on testosterone for nine months, Thomas still referred to him with female pronouns and with his birth name, Kaye. When Thomas was a child, he was particularly close to his grandmother, who was named Kaye. He felt loved and supported by her more than anyone. When he and his wife knew they were having a girl, they were ecstatic. They decided to name their baby girl, Kaye, after his grandmother. Thomas said in therapy that he has seen changes in Kaye. He is aware of her facial

hair and acne, development of a wider neck and bigger biceps, and has listened as her voice become deeper. He said he "took it all in stride" until this weekend when "she" came home with two large masculine-looking tattoos on "her" arm and leg. When Kevin, formerly known as Kaye, came to therapy, he vented his frustration with his dad who continued using "old, dead pronouns and the name Kaye" when referring to him. Kevin feels his dad is not supportive and is "tired of waiting" for him to come around. He hoped his masculine appearance would have made it easier for his dad to accept the change. James is having difficulty letting go.

Another parent reported that she had just received a 10-page letter from her daughter who was a sophomore at an ivy league college saying she had been taking testosterone for 8 months. Enclosed with the letter was a picture of her "daughter" with facial hair, enlarged biceps decorated with masculine looking tattoo's and wearing men's clothes. In the letter, her "daughter" said she was in the process of making a full transition to male. He requested that his mother call him by his new male name with matching pronouns and that she (the mom), "treat me like the male I am."

4) **Your Core Beliefs May be Challenged.**

Your core beliefs about yourself, your child, and sometimes life in general, may now feel as if they are being challenged. You will know this if you find yourself saying, "But it shouldn't be like this" or "This is how things should be going." The "should" is connected to what we learned to be true when we grew up: if you worked hard then there would be a reward, if you were a nice person then others would like you. If you believed in God and led a good life, then your problems would be minimal. We know that this is not true, that you can work hard, be a good person and believe in a higher power, but these things will not guarantee or make you immune from problems or challenges.

Core beliefs and values are the ideas about life that we live by. Maybe you were raised with a binary concept of gender, meaning that people were either male or female. Learning that gender is fluid and there are many different variations people have regarding gender, may not be in your model of "how it's supposed to be." Intersex people, gender variant and other diversities may not have been realities you were aware of as you grew up. Or they were issues that only "others" dealt with. You also may have thought that if you were a good enough parent, this would not be happening. That your child would follow the norm and challenges like this were not something you would have to deal with. Or, you may feel that if you followed your religion faithfully, God would not be sending this your way.

These are irrational beliefs. Challenges come to all of us. All of us have wonderful peak moments in life, memorable experiences, challenges and problems. This is life, and no one is immune. A positive and core value for parents is to think that their child wants their love and approval no matter how old they are, or how successful they are. Hold on to the values in life that support you and help you take the high road to love, peace and understanding. Integrity and serenity will support you while your child is transitioning. Another positive and helpful core belief is that you can find the meaning and love on this journey of parenting, despite challenges.

Many of us have some unresolved core issues. That means that we have issues that resulted in situations that may not have been fair to you in the past, and that still affects you today. Dealing with any resentments or past wounds will help you keep the past from creeping into your child's experience today. Old unresolved wounds can negatively affect the relationship you have with your child today. Parents need support when their core beliefs about their child, themselves or life are being challenged. It also helps parents to heal old unresolved resentments and anger, so these feelings don't get projected onto their child or inside themselves.

Carmen

Carmen struggled, coming from a fundamental religion, to accept that her child was not going to suffer spiritual demise because of being transgender. This was the teaching of the church she had attended for 10 years. Because she was so proud of her 19-year-old daughter and all her accomplishments, Carmen hoped there would be understanding and support from the church. She was devastated to find out, there were neither. Deep down, she felt judged. Carmen knew she would not be treated the same at church if she continued to support her daughter's transition. She was torn between her strong ties to the core beliefs she learned from the church and her cherished role as a loving and supportive mother. After serious thought and in her words "much prayer," she decided to leave her church and find one that was more inclusive, supportive and understanding or her daughter and of her role as a mother who loves and supports her transgender child

5) **Doubting yourself as a parent.**

You did nothing wrong. Being transgender is considered a medical/biological condition. You didn't make your child transgender. No one can make someone transgender. You wouldn't blame yourself if your child had another condition such as diabetes or depression. Every child is different. A parent's job is to give their child a positive sense of self. Therefore, the goal is to understand the symptoms, learn about what transgender means, have each child assessed individually and to make informed decisions that supports the child to be his or her authentic self and have a happy and productive life.

Shame and guilt are feelings that result in us feeling "less than." Guilt is based around action. We may feel guilty because we have done something we regret, or we haven't done something, and we regret that. To overcome guilt, we need to identify the action we need to change, make amends when possible, and do it differently next time.

Shame on the other hand, is about feeling less than, just because we are. Feeling there is something very different and defective about us. That we are less than other people and if they really knew us, they wouldn't like us. Most parents feel they could do more to be a better parent. Most parents get exhausted and overwhelmed with all the responsibilities of being a parent. Some parents don't try enough. Give yourself credit for being a parent and acknowledge all you have done. Give yourself credit for how much you have given of yourself in all you do. Give yourself credit for bringing this child into the world. Give yourself credit for the love you have for your child and for all the memorable moments, experiences, and challenges you have faced together. Trust that this is another challenge in your parenting path. Trust yourself to make a choice to be the kind of parent you want to be while on this path. Remember that success is being the kind of parent you wish you had. You have the choice to be proud of yourself for the way you choose to parent and love your child. Focus on gratitude for all you have, and all you can have in the future.

6) **Concerns about what is best for your child and fear for their safety.**

Parents often have worries about uncertainties and the future. Parents with transgender children worry more. Will my child struggle socially or professionally? Who will love my child? Will they fall in love with someone who won't accept them because they are transgender? Will my child suffer as the victim of bullying, physical violence or hate crimes? Will my child be discriminated against as an adult in terms of employment? You may feel they will be more vulnerable to bullying and non-acceptance in circles familiar to you, i.e. your church, synagogue, your country club. You may think your son is too tall to transition and he will always be a target for attention as a tall woman. You may be worried about putting your minor aged child on hormones, even if you feel a transition is right for them All these are natural and can put more pressure on a parent.

Some parents have concerns regarding hormones. They may feel that their child acted impulsively by going on hormones too soon. Or, that their child was not assessed properly or long enough by the health care provider to know if hormones were in their best interest.

You want what is best for your child. Your opinions and involvement matter. If they are young and there are decisions to be made such as what bathrooms to use at school, or what doctors to go to who are informed about gender, find out all you can and get support. You can be an important part of the decision-making process to facilitate a healthy and safe transition. If your child is older, you can talk to them about steps they are taking towards transitioning and what their ideas are to be and stay safe. Of course, there are no guarantees about safety for anyone, but if your child is old enough to understand safety issues, it's an important topic to discuss together.

7) **You're tired of being "the mean one" or "problem parent" because you have some doubts, which are perceived by your child as not being supportive.**

It takes time to understand all the implications of what it means to have a child with gender dysphoria who wants to make a transition. Not all parents are supportive, especially at first. Parents need time, education and support. You are not "the mean one" or the "problem parent" because you are not immediately on board. Many parents feel that everything they say is wrong even when their intentions are good. Parents deserve to get answers to their questions and to have time to process their feelings. Most parents have many different feelings to work through before they get close to being supportive or accepting. Adjusting takes time.

8) **Dealing with other's reactions and what to tell them.**

Most parents have concerns regarding what others will think and wonder how they will respond when asked about their child. Extended family members, friends, colleagues, the community- how will they react to the news? Common questions parents may ask themselves are: "What will they think of me having a transgender child?", "Will they judge my child unfairly or treat him or her differently?", "Will they judge me as a bad parent because my child is dealing with an issue that is not main stream?", "Was there a problem with my parenting skills?" Parents of transgender children often question themselves. They also may face discrimination and social prejudice simply for standing up for and loving their child.

It can be frightening for a parent to be in the position to deal with other's feelings and reactions, particularly when they are working through their own. It can be especially uncomfortable thinking about how to integrate your child's new identity with people he/she hasn't seen, either during or after transition. This can be particularly hard during holidays, religious rituals and in certain social situation. How to respond to others is addressed in detail in Chapter Seven.

9) **Grieving missed opportunities when your transitioning child is an adult.**

When your child is grown and "comes out," parents sometimes grieve a lifetime of missed childhood opportunities to have bonded with them in their authentic gender.

10) **Dealing with Loss of Control.**

Depending on the age of the child, some parents try to control the situation by having control over the child. This might come out in unreasonable requests and demands:

"I want you to quit attending the LGBT support group. You can do what you want after high school, but not now."

"If you don't stay in college and graduate as a boy/girl, I will stop paying for it."

"You can do what you want when you're out of my house, but while you live here, you will be a boy/girl." (Birth sex)

"Just go to the prom as a boy, so I can have one last picture/celebration, with you as a boy."

These demands don't put parents in control but will more likely push their child away, resulting in the parent feeling more detached. Controlling is a direct response to our fear, panic and sense of helplessness. The way to regain control is to focus on you and replace control with trust. Trust in yourself that you will listen and cope with all that your child brings your way. Trust that there is meaning in everything and that you will find meaning in this too. Trust that you could have an outcome that surpasses your expectations. Trust that when problems appear, you will have the resources necessary to solve them. You can let go of your need to control and become peaceful and calm.

11) **It's easier to focus on your child's feelings - not yours.**

Another issue that makes it hard for parents is that it is always easier to focus on your child. You have years of focusing on their needs and issues. If they are a minor, their issues seem more pressing, more immediate. It's your job to not only meet their needs, but often anticipate what their needs will be. This means putting your child's needs first. Because parents are used to thinking of their child first, it is easy to continue to do this as they get older and particularly when they are transitioning. This makes it easy to overlook your needs, feelings and health.

You may think you don't have time to deal with your feelings. That there are things that need to be done and you need to take control. No matter what the age of your child, there may be pressing issues that you feel need to be dealt with immediately. Feeling stressed or pressured can make you feel like you have too much to do to focus on your feelings. But, no matter what the pressing issues are that you are facing, parents need to take care of themselves. By doing so, you will cope more effectively. Now that you are told they are transgender and may want to transition, you have a multitude of questions concerning their well-being. All these questions are valid. But taking care of you is the foundation to taking care of your child and the issues at hand.

12) **Other stressors.**

Sometimes this news comes at a time when you may have other stressors that you were already dealing with. Bob came to therapy because in the last six months he lost both his parents, got laid off from his job and now his 17-year-old son has told him he is transgender. Challenges can seem unsurmountable when they come at the same time. Parents may have other issues to deal with that are unresolved or bothering them simultaneously.

Grief, Anticipatory Grief, Transition Grief

Grief

Grief is a process that helps us move from our past, into today, and into the future. It helps us move to acceptance. It is cleansing and healing.

Grief comes when you feel something is altered or is gone forever, and often without your consent. It leaves us dealing with the mix of emotions that comes from change, when that change is connected to a real or a perceived loss. Grief ebbs and flows like an ocean. It takes time to see land again after the big wave comes over you. We learn to swim and do whatever we need, to stay afloat. It is not self-indulgent. It is survival. It is not a normal state. It is a transitional state. To get through it, we often have to rely on our emergency power to manage daily life. The changes you experience while your child transitions can leave you in grief. You are aware there are going to be changes, which bring to an end, some things that you know and love now. For example, there will be the obvious change in outward appearance and gender identity and gender expression, including hair, body shape, facial changes, clothing and attitude. There will be changes with the friends they choose, and loss of using their birth name. You may be asked to treat them differently, even if it means giving up things you used to enjoy doing together. You may not be able to have future time with your child in the gender in which you have raised them. You may not be able to call them by their "old name"- commonly referred to as their "dead name," which may have had sentimental meaning to you. There may be loss for the changes this makes to the family dynamics as they stand now, and loss of the future dreams you had for watching them grow up in their birth sex. There may be added loss of any dreams you may have had for you together in their birth sex. You are grieving what will not come to be.

During grief, transition, transformation, change, we are not always clear about what we are experiencing or why. That is because we cannot see the whole picture. We are limited to a small focus. We may feel physically weak or small and experience a mental lack of clarity. We need to know that this confusion is temporary. We need to not stress ourselves trying to figure it all out while we're grieving. Things will make sense later. We need to accept we are in a transition ourselves and that our understanding of things will become clearer with time.

Adapting to change and loss is a process. It can be draining and exhausting and wear your down. You may feel more tired than usual. You may feel that you

cannot function well in other areas of your life. Some
people find themselves hiding out in the safety of their
bedroom or another safe space. It's okay to be gentle
with yourself. You don't have to expect more than you
can deliver at this time. You may even expect less than
you would normally. Know that all these feelings are
temporary although it may not feel like it at the time.
Trust that you will feel better. In the meantime, you do
not have to control, understand and plan everything.
You cannot accomplish anything more quickly by
acting out of a sense of fear, frustration, sadness or
urgency. Trust in yourself. The way will become clear
and you will know what to do in time.

Even the most loving parent,
requires a period of adjustment,
when dealing with grief.

Grieving is lonely. We live in a culture that doesn't
know how to grieve. We live in a society that wants
us to get back to normal as soon as possible. Society
wants us to keep moving and get on with our lives.
When a friend is grieving, friends and relatives may
be uncomfortable seeing someone they love in pain.
They don't know what to say. They may detach
because they fear it will happen to them. When a
child transitions, parents grieve. They feel the loss
of the relationship they have with their child in the

gender they know them to be. They feel apart from other parents who are not going through this with their child. They feel pressure to keep up with work, raising other siblings and managing their other various responsibilities, while going through a loss that may be hard to speak about.

> *The more you identify or are connected to a loved one,*
> *and the gender to which they live now,*
> *the harder it can be to accept a change.*

Grief is work. Avoiding it can be more work. Let yourself give in to the healing power of grief. With time, the pain subsides. The power of grief can soften your feelings and heal your heart with compassion and patience.

Marjorie
Marjorie raised her daughter Kim as a single parent. Since Kim was a gifted soprano, Marjorie sacrificed by taking extra jobs so that Kim could take singing lessons throughout grammar and high school. Although she worked quite a bit, Marjorie made an effort to keep an emotionally close relationship with her daughter through open communication and by being there for her as much as she could. Her daughter was her main priority in life. Kim sang at Carnegie Hall when she was 15 and at 17 was on television for "America's Got Talent." Her family and friends, especially Marjorie, had great hopes for her future

as a singer. As a result, she received a music scholarship to
a prestigious university to continue to study voice.
Marjorie felt their relationship continued to be close, even
when Kim was at the university. In the middle of the
second semester of her sophomore year in college, Marjorie
received a 10-page letter from her daughter. It said she was
on testosterone, which is a masculinizing hormone. It
facilitates many physical changes as well as permanently
changing a female voice, to a deeper more masculine voice.
She also said she was in the process of getting a name and
gender change and would be living full-time as a male
within four months. Marjorie felt their "emotionally
close" relationship was shattered. She felt used having
sacrificed for so many years for Kim to have voice lessons
and betrayed that Kim didn't confide in her about her
feelings earlier. To say the least, Marjorie was devastated
and overwhelmed with grief.

Grief can also come to those who are happy about
transition. Sometimes in divorce, the person who
initiated the split discovers a day when they are just
sad, and they don't know why. Even though they
wanted the divorce, they still may be grieving the
future and the dreams they once thought they were
going to have. Even parents who are happy and
relieved that their child has found an answer to their
pain, grieve the loss of their child in the gender they
are used to.

Alma

Alma, a 46-year-old mother, came to therapy with her 14-year-old son, Trey. Trey was born female. Trey had been telling his mother he was a male since early childhood and was now a sophomore in high school. Alma and Trey both walked in smiling. Alma began the session with, "We're here so you can help my son make a legal and medical transition, so he can live as the male that he is. I am ready to support him in any way I can. I see how unhappy he is being forced to live as a girl, and to me he has been just as much of a son as his brothers since he was born." Trey wanted to have "top surgery" (breast removal and male chest contouring) and have a legal name change. He wanted to transition and change schools between sophomore and junior year, so he could finish his last two years of high school as a male. Trey's step-father was supportive, but his biological father was not. It took several months of family therapy with his biological father, before he was able to understand the anguish Trey lived with daily, and why Trey felt transitioning was essential for his survival. Trey was eventually able to meet his goals and had top surgery and a legal name change. His changes happened later than what he wanted, but he was able to transition between senior year and college. Trey and his family are very pleased with his transition.

When talking to Alma about her journey, she claims that although she feels certain that transitioning was best for

him, she related that "in the beginning" it was hard for
her to give up the idea of having a daughter. Holding on
to the idea of wanting what was best for him, helped her
welcome the change and adapt.

Anticipatory Grief

Anticipation can magnify the emotions associated
with an event. When we anticipate a holiday,
celebration or vacation, the excitement is enhanced
just thinking of what will come. We may not know
what will happen, but we anticipate a positive
experience which results in feeling good. This
projection is similar in anticipatory grief, but it
doesn't feel positive. Anticipatory Grief is what you
feel *before* the loss or perceived loss occurs.
Anticipatory Grief is grieving about things to come,
fear of the unknown. Most of the time in grief, we
are focused on the loss in the past, but in
anticipatory grief, we focus on the change and loss
ahead. With a transitioning child, Anticipatory Grief
makes parents wonder about things to come. For
example: What will our relationship be like now and
after transition? What will it be like living without
my son/ daughter as I know them now? How will
this change our family dynamics? How will we
handle holidays and family celebrations? What will I
tell people? How will this change any social or
professional opportunities for our child? How will

this affect other siblings once they find out? How will transitioning affect their appearance? Will we be discriminated against because of transition? Anticipatory Grief is about anticipating the unknown of a perceived loss resulting in stress, anxiety and/or sadness.

Robert
Robert, a 43-year-old financial advisor was the only child born to a prestigious family from a big city. Growing up, he and his father enjoyed activities together such as watching sports, going hunting and discussing finances. Robert had a thriving successful business as a financial advisor. He served in the military and had an MBA from Harvard. His family had him manage the bulk of their estate. Robert moved to another big city, telling his family he was taking time for himself. In reality, he was transitioning and afraid to tell his parents. He told them four months after he began taking hormones and was living full-time as a female. When they found out, they were stricken with grief. They couldn't imagine losing their only son. They had tremendous Anticipatory Grief wondering what was going to become of Robert. Would he be safe living as a female, how could they live without "him," would his clients drop him, would this be the demise of his business, what would they tell their friends? They were grieving the loss of their son, but also experienced a great deal of anticipatory grief, trying to envision and anticipate what was to come.

Transition Grief

Transition grief is the personal loss one feels, having to let go of the relationship as one knew it, prior to someone they know who makes a gender transition.

This is not limited to family members, but to anyone who is experiencing loss, related to the relationship they have with someone who is transitioning.

Parents often relate transition to death, even though their child is alive and well. Yet, it is the ending of the gender they have known their child to be. The gender in which they imagined a future. Although the child is beginning a new chapter in a new gender, they too carry memories and experiences of the past.

Parents of transgender children experience grief, anticipatory grief, and transition grief, simultaneously.

You have not lost your past. The love, the joys, the celebrations, the good times and the struggles that you have shared are not lost. Neither are the parenting accomplishments, milestones and memories. You can cherish them always and use them as a source of strength anytime you'd like. All you sacrificed and gave to your child while parenting remains valid and worthwhile. Honor your character and your life by cherishing these precious memories. Your child is changing his/her gender. Although they do not relate anymore to their previous gender, it does not mean they didn't benefit or appreciate all you did for them at that time. They may not cherish thinking of themselves in the old gender or with their former name, but this does not mean all you did for them at that time was not important. Having contributed to making them who they are is extremely important and is significant for them and for you.

Any grief reminds us of our ability to care and to love. If we didn't care, we wouldn't hurt.

With transitioning children, parents grieve the life they thought we were going to have with their child. We can, in time, appreciate, cherish and love the times we had, release our grip on the life we thought we were going to have, and choose to accept the different something new. Grief heals pain, so we can go forward and love the child who is in front of us. Value yourself for being flexible and able to adapt. Value your spouse or primary relationship. Don't let this put distance between you. An open attitude not only keeps us open to unlimited opportunities, it creates a space to experience what may be even better than what we are able to imagine.

Ask yourself the following questions, to see how you have handled grief in the past:

o   Was handling loss taught to you and role modeled as a child?

o   Was what you were taught about loss and grief the same as what you experienced?

o   Are you confident in your ability to cope? Do you have confidence with your skills to deal with the unexpected?

o   Do you live with disappointment thinking you did not handle a change or loss well in the past?

You are never the same person after grieving a loss. The benefit is that things get crystal clear regarding what is important and who is important to you. It remodels us with greater strengths and compassion. After loss we are processed into a new life and don't have to fear loss. Loss teaches us that we can transform ourselves. Grief enables us to go forward and get to the other side until we can unfold our wings and fly again.

It can be particularly hard to deal with grief if you grew up with losses that no one discussed, or if there was no one to model how to deal with loss and grief. Today, there are books, workshops, support groups and webinars, all focused on helping people understand and work through their grief. Resources are available when you feel ready to take that next step.

Chapter 2
Can I handle this?

*At every moment, we have the ability to
choose how we react to every situation with
the decision to stop doing whatever it is that
sabotages our potential to manifest
a fulfilling life.*

Choices

C an you deal with this? Not only can you deal
with it, but you can benefit from it. There will be
opportunities you experience that can add to your own
personal growth as well as add to a happy relationship
with your child, if you let it. When you brought this
little soul into the world, you had no idea what was to
come. But you probably felt you would deal with
anything. You knew you would step up to the
challenge, even though you didn't know what the
journey was going to be like. We are all here with a
purpose. Part of yours is to be a parent.

Having a transgender child can be challenging. If
your child is young, living with you or if you have a
close relationship with them, you too are now an

active part of the changes that will be happening. Their changes will affect your life. Accepting this reality is about making choices and moving forward. Parents need to choose:

1) How they want to react to their child being transgender and

2) How they want to let this reality affect them. You can choose to see your child as "the problem," or you can deal with the challenges, work through them and create positive results.

You can see your child as "the problem," or you can deal with the challenges, work though them and create positive results.

Three choices parents often use to cope are:

1) **Staying stuck or immobile**. This is where we lose connection with our life. We don't grow or live to the fullest. The feeling of being lost becomes normal.
2) **Sabotage**. This manifests with all kinds of self-defeating behaviors. Parents can make it worse with drugs, alcohol, other addictions or behaviors that defeat moving forward.
3) **Resilience**. This is where we put the pieces together and become whole. Where we stop

looking OK on the outside and feel broken on the inside. Resilience doesn't mean you didn't live with a shock. It means realizing that even in our grief, we can come back to the part that makes us feel like ourselves. Where things get better and we start believing again in our uniqueness our strengths, our life. Eventually, you know it's time to start something new, and trust the magic of new beginnings.

Ask yourself the following questions to help you connect with yourself and assess how you are doing:

1) How have I chosen to handle this so far? (Staying stuck, Sabotage, Resilience, other)

2) Is it working for me?

3) Are my choices supporting both my child and myself?

4) Is there anything I would like to be doing differently?

5) What needs to happen, so I can reconnect with myself and have a productive, happy life?

6) Have there been any changes with my child's transition that I have dealt with so far, that have worked out better than I expected?

Overall, the ironic thing is that despite what you say and do, children will be who they are. We want them to take all the good we can give them and integrate it to their own destiny. Sometimes this happens and sometimes it doesn't. But like all human beings, they are here to follow their own journey and lead their own path. Parents can guide, but they can't control or change their child to be someone they are not.

Any parent with a healthy child can rejoice that this is so. Some children aren't as fortunate. Those with children who are dying, disabled or living with a chronic illness face difficult challenges. Sometimes children live with hardships that offer no relief. Addiction, life-threatening illnesses, limited mental abilities, learning disabilities and mood disorders are challenges we can manage but not always eliminate. Being transgender is not an illness. It is a condition. A condition that can be dealt with successfully. People can transition socially, medically or both, with excellent results. Transgender people can have productive, successful, happy, healthy lives. That is what healthy parents want most for their child.

Do you really *want* to struggle? Do you *have* to struggle? Is that how you deal with other problems? Can you still call it a good day even things don't always work out as you planned? Do you have days where you do 10 things right but stay awake, thinking of the one thing you could have done differently? Can you look at the overall picture? Do you procrastinate until the last minute and then pressure yourself to get something done? Sometimes we have habits that limit us. Sometimes we make it harder than it has to be. As a parent, do you have to be the unhappy one? Eventually you will want to let go of the struggle and move to peace and clarity. It begins with knowing what you can change and what you can't and knowing the difference between the two.

An important thing to remember, is that being transgender is not a choice. It is a need for some because they cannot go on living in the body they have now or because they cannot continue to live in excruciating pain, being treated continually as the person they are not. They cannot live in a world where others have expectations of them that do not fit who they are and expectation that they cannot relate to. It is not an easy road to transition. When I have commented to clients that I respect the courage it takes to make the changes they are making, the response is often the same, "I didn't have a choice."

You are still the parent

Transition doesn't mean that you can't continue to enjoy parenting or that your role has diminished in value. You are still the parent and are more important than ever. There will be many issues your child will be facing. If your child is young, you may be the one to make decisions about social and medical transitioning. This might include decisions about hormones, what kind of clothing to buy, who to tell, when to tell, etc. It may also involve letting significant people in your child's life know about their gender issues, or transition if applicable. If they are older and can make their own decisions, your thoughts and feedback may be critically important to them. You are the parent and a major support in your child's life. Your child's success and mental health will be affected by your reaction and how you treat them. Parent reactions and behavior affect their child's self-image, self-worth and self-confidence.

You are important. Your feelings are important. You are still the parent and together you can continue to build and enjoy a wonderful relationship with deep compassion and love. If you need support, there is plenty available. Trust yourself. You probably know more than you think you do and can handle change better than you think you can. Be kind to yourself and know that you are in a process. You are letting go of the way some things used to be. You may find yourself resisting to change, resistant to change your trusted and familiar path. Ask yourself, "What if I had a willingness, an openness to see things another way?" What do I really want for my child and what am I willing to let go of to have it? Even if you don't understand what is happening, try and trust the process and imagine that the new behaviors, ideas and awareness will emerge with time. And in time, you can have a life that you can love.

Ask yourself:

1) Do I appreciate myself and my role as a parent?

2) What internal needs does parenting satisfy for me?

3) What is it I love about being a parent?

4) Do I see my role as a parent a part of my purpose in life?

5) How does knowing that being transgender is not a choice, affect the way you see your child?

6) Is this something you would like to discuss more in detail with your child?

7) Where and with whom are you getting your support?

8) What things in your life help you stay grounded, healthy and inspired?

9) What would it take to imagine that your child transitions and it all works out?

These questions are to help you become aware of your reactions, behaviors and feelings when asking yourself if you can handle the situation. After answering, ask yourself if your responses match the way you see yourself and the way you want to be? If not, what do you need to do to make changes? Balance comes when our behaviors and actions match up with how we see ourselves.

There may be times when you need to slow down and relax your mind. Where you make deliberate, conscious efforts to take a little more time to do what you love and notice the beauty around you. A time to be grateful for the things in your life that you love. Showing kindness, living peacefully and not letting others manipulate you, will help you maintain your serenity. If you have faith, rely on the gifts it can give you by helping you remember who you really are. When you are balanced, you can be more productive and more at peace. This can help keep things associated with transitioning more workable and in perspective. Taking care of you will put you in a better position physically, emotionally, and spiritually to deal with the issues at hand.

Life Doesn't Have to be Perfect to be Wonderful

It is not unusual to think that anyone gets through life without facing an unwanted and unexpected challenge that changes our lives forever. Some people face many. Events can challenge and change our vision, our reality and our dream of how we thought our lives were going to be. It is not only by having a transgender child. What about the woman who grows up dreaming of having several children, but then is told by her gynecologist that she has uterine cancer and needs an immediate hysterectomy? What about the triathlete who at 43-years old is told he has 4th stage brain cancer? Or, the 14-year-old son who came home from school only to find out his best friend, his dad, unexpectedly died of a heart attack that day, or, finding out after 30 years of marriage that your husband not only is having an affair and wants a divorce, but that his new girlfriend just had his baby? No one expects these things will happen to them, but they do, and they happen to all of us. Handling change and loss, is part of living that we experience regularly throughout our entire life. Sometimes it is through these incidences that we deepen our understanding of what is important and what we truly value in life. When challenged, we learn to deal with losses, and go on. We learn we can live through all of it. We learn to find meaning. We learn to put things into perspective. We may even see characteristics that we didn't know we had. We grow. We learn to thrive. Parents of transgender children have an amazing opportunity to show what being a loving parent really means. At the same time, they have an opportunity to develop a multitude of strengths, skills and compassion that results in valuing themselves in the process.

Acceptance is about acknowledging and accepting the loss and learning to take energy from that loss and move forward with peace, contentment and joy. Acceptance is where you leave the crisis behind and experience a sense of empowerment. It doesn't mean the challenges are over, but that you can move on and enjoy life. You have a child to love who needs you. You have purpose. You have a future.

Helpful Tips to Take Care of You

1) Asking "Why Me?" will not help. You don't need to understand *why* this is happening right now, just that it *is* happening. You may have

seen signs or not. Don't try to blame or find reasons to justify it.

2) Know that things won't feel normal for a while and that is OK. This stage will pass eventually and then you will deal with things you don't feel up to now.

3) When you find yourself obsessed with thoughts about your child, particularly on things you cannot change, temporarily redirect your focus to you. Try to get centered on what you need to do today. Do what you do to stay balanced and grounded. Meditating, yoga, exercise, hobbies, listen to music, play music, dance, call friends, go to a movie, the theatre, watch or participate in sports, walk, run, spend time with your pet, go to a park, go to the beach, etc. If you haven't done any of the above, you may want to start. We all need to "escape" our feelings of overwhelm at times. Doing something to shift the energy can give you the break you may need to rebalance and feel peace.

4) Try not to overact. You have a million unanswered questions. Worries are understandable, but there will be answers. You need time to adjust and put all this into perspective. But for now, attend to your day-to-

day activities and do what you would normally do. Take it one day at a time.

5) Until you feel more like yourself, don't force yourself to do anything you don't want to do or make any major decisions.

6) Delegate when possible. Can you delegate some of your responsibilities? Can you delegate at work? Can you refrain from taking on any new projects/clients for a while? Get a housekeeper? Do you need help or support to keep going? The idea is to keep functioning and keep up with your usual responsibilities, but not be on overload. Doing too much can be a way to avoid dealing with your feelings.

7) Find someone you trust and feel safe with where you can be totally honest and share all your feelings. Grieving can be lonely, especially when you feel you are the only one going through it. What you are experiencing can be healing to share. Find someone who will listen and allow you to be exactly where you are. You may wish to speak with a professional counselor who has expertise with transition. If you are not ready at this point to talk to anyone, that is OK. You can when you are ready. Parents reach out for support and therapy at all stages.

8) If your child thinks he/she is transgender, make sure he/she has a supportive, educated therapist or counselor well versed in gender issues. Training and experience are essential. Do not be afraid you are "encouraging them" to be transgender by giving them a safe place to speak openly about their feelings. You are being a good parent.

9) Give yourself permission to grieve even if you have a natural resistance to showing or feeling your feelings. Know that there is no correct way to do it and no way you "should" feel at this time. You feel as you feel. But you need to step into it, get to know it and live with it, to eventually get through it. Know that your body will take the time it needs to get you to a more comfortable and more stable place. Don't let others make you think you need to "suck it up", "move on" or that it's "no big deal." They may be trying to minimize dealing with their own feelings or they don't know what else to say. Remember: It's your child and your life. You are important and it's a big deal to you.

10) Identify any past loss and explore how it was handled. If you feel you are ready, find a trusted person or counselor who can explore this with

you and help you work through your feeling of loss.

11) You can speak your truth to your child and be honest with him/ her, but don't minimize or shame them for their feelings. Transitioning has its challenges for everyone in the family. For the child, it is always easier with support and understanding from a loving parent. Being there, on the level that is comfortable for you, does not only make your child's journey easier but can give you the satisfaction of feeling that you are an essential part of your child's life at this important time. You have a choice to be an essential and important part of the process but if you are not ready, say so, and tell them you want to be supportive, but you need more time.

12) Know that your child may not be able to empathize with you if you perceive transitioning as a loss. To them transition is a huge, positive gain. It's the opportunity to live for the first time, being themselves. The first time they can act and be seen for who they truly are. They are looking for the comfort they see in other people who can react naturally as to who they truly are. For them, transitioning offers freedom. It also offers the opportunity that maybe for the first time, they can be who they truly are and be treated

accordingly. Without this, they are subject to living a life that is not their own, full of pretense, shame and misery. Always hiding their authentic self because they are trapped in a body that does not represent who they are. Trapped in a body where the world is judging them on how they look on the outside. Trapped because the world has expectations that their feelings match the way they look. Therefore, your child will fail because these expectations are unrealistic to who they truly are. Not being able to transition can be the difference between life, and emotional and sometimes physical death.

13) It may be helpful to try and separate your job as a parent if you have initial misgivings about your child's transition. You may have unresolved feelings about the transition at this point, but you are still a parent. You can still be the nurturing parent you were before. You don't have to give up the things that made you feel like a good parent. You can still create love, support, safety and be nurturing. That doesn't necessarily mean you understand and approve of the transition, it means you are still a loving parent.

14) Remember that you want your child to be happy and live their life to the fullest. You also need to be happy and live your life to the fullest. Don't forget that you are responsible for making your life work and for your own happiness. Even if you don't think you want this to happen, remind yourself that you want your child to live the best life possible. Try and be open to that, even if you're unsure of the outcome. Some of life's greatest experiences come from unexpected events.

15) *When you are ready*, try and talk with your child about what transgender means to them. You may also want to do some reading about gender dysphoria, gender identity, gender nonconformity, and transition. You might want to learn the different terms associated with transition and what they mean. Learn the difference between sexual orientation and gender identity. Learn that being male or female are not the only categories for gender. Learn about intersex, gender queer, non-binary identities and more. You and your child will have more to talk about and it will facilitate understanding where you can both use the same language. This will also empower you should transgender issues come up in any other conversations or situations.

16) Keep a daily journal. Writing will help you express your feelings and work through them. It may be interesting to date each time you write, so you can see how your feelings change with time. Later, you will have a great documentation and record of your experience and all you went through.

17) If you have a faith that helps you, connect with it. Faith at this point, may mean to believe that this is happening for a reason. Maybe there is a higher purpose and plan at play. One that is better than you could have imagined. Spirituality supports us to feel positive and worthy of love and gives us healthy perspectives to view life and the world. Faith can help us see a bigger picture of ourselves and our purpose.

18) Remember to think about and be mindful of what you are grateful for in your life. There is plenty of good all around you. Let your trust in the good be a stabilizing part of your life. Know that things will feel better eventually and that it is always possible to heal and go forward. You are on a new journey. Be open to any positive events that could result from it. Live in the present and take one day at a time and remember that your life is a gift.

19) Take time to acknowledge YOU, all you do, all you have accomplished in your life, all the love and kindness you have given others, all the love and kindness you have received from others. Be grateful for the people who have supported you in your life.

20) Be grateful for being a parent. For all the sacrifices you have made and all the memories you have as a parent. Some people never had the choice to have their own children. Free yourself from any guilt and judgement and focus on gratitude. Your child is a precious gift who has much to offer. Don't forget you still have a child to love and who needs you.

21) Know that parenting is still something you can value, enjoy and cherish. Know that the parenting you do and your relationship with your child can continue to give insight, wisdom and happiness. Stay open to the process.

Chapter 3

Dealing with Feelings

"Real power comes from allowing ourselves to be vulnerable enough to feel hurt. Real power comes from knowing we can take care of ourselves, even when we feel emotional pain. Real power comes when we stop holding others responsible for our pain and we take responsibility for all our feelings."

- Melody Beattie "The Language of Letting Go"

P arents can go through a mix of feelings throughout their child's transition. Some parents feel uncomfortable dealing with their child's gender issues and some feel   transition makes it even more complicated. They see it as an unwelcomed, undeserved and unwanted problem. Some parents feel they are to blame. Some feel guilty because they cannot readily offer the child the love and support they are so used to giving. Others are angry about   having to tell others. Some have shame that others will judge them as bad parents. Some parents feel insecure or inadequate and judge themselves for feeling they failed or are not good enough or this wouldn't have happened.

To be more prepared to deal with your feelings, ask yourself the following:

1) What is your level of comfort when dealing with your feelings?

2) How do you experience anger, pain, loss, vulnerability and lack of control?

3) What were the messages you grew up with regarding these feelings and emotions?

4) How did your family deal with feelings in general?

5) How did you learn to process your emotions as a child? How does that work for you today?

6) How comfortable are you dealing with someone else's anger, sadness or depression?

7) Is there anything else you might be angry, sad or depressed about?

8) Are there other issues in your life that you were actively dealing with prior to being told about your child's transition?

If so, some of those feelings may be projected on to your child, particularly if they are unresolved.

Denial

"Mom, Dad, I'm a girl".
"Mom, Dad, I'm a boy".

What happens when your unique and precious child who you have given a lifetime of unconditional love and support, challenges you with the fact that he/she is transgender? Most parents have little skill and understanding about how to deal with their child "coming out" as transgender, but they know what they feel. Often parents feel shock. To protect ourselves from a shock, we often go into denial. Denial is a physical and emotional altered state. It feels like numbness or even mental paralysis. Parent's find themselves saying, "Is this really true?" "I can't believe this." A big part of your world stops while everything continues around you. The world looks surreal. You're in disbelief. You lose touch with yourself. You say you're OK, but your heart feels shattered. Denial is about not letting ourselves face reality because facing it seems unbearable. Denial is meant to protect us.

*Denial is our body's way of helping
us manage our feelings and avoid
dealing with the pain.*

It's nature's way of letting in only what we can handle. We deal with the reality of the situation in our own time, when we are ready. We are ready when we are safe and strong enough to deal with the truth.

Some parents may not be in denial but still feel sadness or grief. Grief is about dealing with a loss even if you are OK with the outcome. People who initiate a divorce, often have a period where they grieve the hopes and dreams they had previously. They may be grieving the dreams they had when they got married. They grieve what is not coming to fruition. Some parents are relieved that their child has found an answer to their sadness. Some parents may even be positive regarding transition, yet they too can feel grief. Grief that you won't be able to see your child get older and have the experiences you thought you once would have with them in the gender you know them now. You grieve the loss of the experiences, rituals and rites of passage that come with parenthood and seeing your child grow up. The truth is that you can still share many experiences, rituals, create memories to cherish, but they will be in your child's authentic gender.

Having feelings isn't being weak- it's being alive. Our feelings are connected to our values and beliefs. What do your feelings tell you about you? Have you experienced and overcome any other situation that were unexpected and wanted initially? How did you manage and cope with that? Reflect on how you overcame that and ask if in the long run it has changed your life for the better.

Parent Emotions/Questions/Reactions

"I never thought he/she was this unhappy."

Because of the fear of rejection, many children (minor or adult) keep their feelings to themselves. Most don't share their feelings particularly if they were taught that not conforming meant pain, isolation or ridicule. Some wait trying to avoid negative responses. Some wait because they fear it will put stress on the parents or the family. Some wait until they think the outcome will be understood. Others come out even when they feel acceptance will be a problem, because the pain of living in pretense, as someone who they are not, becomes unbearable. Children do not want to burden their parents. Not facing reality and speaking up about it means living a lifetime of pretense and misery. Standing up to the truth is hard to do, but an act of courage. Most hold back when they think someone will minimize their pain, tell them to get over it, talk about them behind their back with judgement or ridicule, or worse, abandon them.

"She seemed to enjoy being a girl" or "He seemed to enjoy being a boy."

What if one day your "girly-girl" daughter, who you felt enjoyed wearing make-up, liked wearing dresses, had an active lifestyle congruent with all the expectations society would have with being female, comes out and tells you that she is a boy and has a plan to begin taking testosterone soon. Some parents have daughters that present as more gender neutral or as a "tomboy." But with no indication or signs that their daughter felt like or wanted to be a man, a parent may be left with confusion and doubt that this is the right thing for her.

Or you may have a history of seeing your son, who appeared to enjoy stereotypical male activities for most of his life who one day comes out and says he is a female. This can be very confusing particularly if you shared in the male activities and feel you witnessed genuine enjoyment and happiness first hand. Some children did enjoy their previous history of living as their biological sex. Some of their feelings were authentic. On the other hand, some did what was expected, some didn't know how to express when they weren't comfortable as a boy or girl and some didn't identify their transgender identity until much later. Either way, it can be confusing for a parent.

How to Help Yourself Through Denial

Know that you may have many unanswered questions at this time, and your questioning is understandable. Questions about how this happened, what happened, issues about your child, issues about others, issues concerning yourself. *You don't need to have all the answers at this time.* Eventually, you will find out more information on gender identity, transgender issues and your child's specific individual needs. At this stage, just notice your own feelings and reactions and follow the steps listed at the end of Chapter 2, to take care of you.

What to Say to Your Child

"I did not know you were going through so much for all this time. Can you tell me more about it?"

"I feel like I have so much to learn about this–
please be patient with me."

"I'd like to be supportive, but I don't feel it yet.
Please give me more time."

"You are important to me, but I'm not ready to
accept all of this yet."

"You have been dealing with this longer than I have
- I need more time."

"Please be patient with me."

"Can we talk about this together as a family?"

"I may need some time to understand and learn
what this means for you, me and our family."

"I'm glad you told me."

"I don't know what I'm going to say to others."

"This is a big adjustment for me."

"I love you no matter what gender you are."

"You can count on me to be here for you."

"I'd like for you to talk to me more about what you
are going through."

What Not to Say

"I don't think this is how you should feel."

"You're being influenced by the wrong people."

"Your feelings will pass." "It's probably a stage."

"I feel so guilty, it's all my fault."

"How can you think you will ever look good enough to pass as a woman/man?"

More suggestions:

Don't blame them, yourself or anyone else for their need to transition.

Don't talk at your child, talk with him/her.

"If only" and "What if" are always dead ends.

You can feel more in control by focusing on the present and taking care of you.

Depression

Understanding Depression

Grieving the loss of your child in the gender you have known them puts some parents in a depressed state. Depression keeps us protected by shutting down our nervous system, so we have time to adapt to something we feel we cannot handle. It will leave when it has served its purpose.

When people talk about depression, they tend to express it as a feeling, such as: "I feel heavy and lethargic." "I feel like I'm swimming through molasses." "I feel like I have 50 pounds on my shoulders all the time." "I feel like there's a black cloud over my head and wherever I go, it follows me." Some report that it feels like a withdrawal from life that leaves them in a fog of sadness. We know that when depressed, life can feel hopeless and meaningless.

The five symptoms of clinical depression are:

1) Over eating or under eating, (gaining or losing over 15 pounds in the last six months),

2) Over sleeping or under sleeping, (sleeping significantly more or less than your usual amount in the last six months),

3) Feeling more tearful and emotional in general,

4) Having difficulty focusing and/or concentrating,

5) Feeling numb when it comes to partying or socializing. Feeling that if you were socializing and celebrating, you wouldn't feel the spark of having fun.

If you have 2-3 of these symptoms and they have lasted for several weeks, you may want to seek professional advice from a psychiatrist or therapist.

Depression often results from loss. Some people have inherited a tendency to get depressed and therefore become depressed easier than others because of their genetics. (Endogenous depression). Others can get depressed due to external situations that result in loss. (Exogenous or situational depression). Some people experience both. Either way, it's important to treat and manage depression early, so you can feel better as soon as possible.

For some people, depression is not a mental illness but an appropriate response to loss. Not feeling sad would be unusual when feeling a loss. Parents can have several losses to grieve when their child transitions. They may be grieving the loss of the present role they have with their child. They may be grieving aspects of family life and activities they did together. Parents may seriously be grieving their "old" self, the person they were before they knew anything was about to change.

Some people get relief taking anti-depressants if they have multiple symptoms that linger or get worse. Reach out for help and support if you need it. The goal is to feel better and return to your previous level of functioning as soon as possible.

You may feel as if all you have ever done for your child does not matter. But it does, and you will feel all that again when your depression has passed. In time you won't feel so alone. As time goes on, you may see things differently than you do now. You may find positive aspects of your child's transition for both you and your child. Your world may get bigger with the things you learn and the new contacts you make along the way. You may even come to appreciate the changes you see your child making in their new life.

How to Help Yourself Through Depression

If you have a history of depression and feel you are getting depressed again, see your doctor, a psychiatrist or psychotherapist. Discuss options to get help. Assess your alcohol and substance use (if any). Don't use alcohol or substances to self-medicate. Although they may provide temporary relief, it is only temporary. Using substances will only prolong working through your feelings. They can also sabotage your ability to feel alive, to face your situation and to find solutions. Depression will go away in time but can often go away faster with the right medication. See your doctor to assess if anti-depressants can help you. In addition, some people focus on good nutrition, exercise, acupuncture, meditation, certain herbs, yoga, tai chi, etc., to help feel better. Talk to your health care specialists to see what other alternatives might also work for you.

Introverts tend to hold their feelings inside while extroverts tend to "let it all out." If you hold all your feelings inside and tend to keep them to yourself, you might want to think about how much easier this could be with support by someone who understands and cares. This could be a grief group, support group, ideally, a support group for parents of transgender children, a psychotherapist, another parent of a trans child, or a trusted friend who would understand and want to support you. Most introverts tend to feel uncomfortable going to a group event alone. Ask someone you trust to go with you. If you're an extrovert, you may find it easier to find the support you need and may be more comfortable going alone. Either way, it's always easier to go through any challenge with support and compassion from others.

Those who care about you will want to hear from you and will want to be there for you. You will also see that not everyone will be comfortable with the news. When that happens, know that their feelings are about them, not you or your child. You may be mad at friends or family members who aren't empathetic and who don't understand your loss. They may come around in time. In the meantime, you can get what you need and take care of yourself. You are the one who can heal your loss. There are many other people who can and will support you on your journey. You do not have to feel alone.

When you are ready, reach out for support. Reaching out is a sign of strength and good self-esteem. You will come out of this stage in time but a kind, compassionate and informed listener can make it easier. They will remind you of your strengths and guide you to stay centered and grounded.

Above all, remember, you have a child to love and from whom you can get love in return. You have a purpose. You are still a parent and an important part of their life. They are still an important part of yours. You will feel better. You will reconnect with time. Be kind to yourself and give yourself time to heal. You will eventually see that family life and parenting can still be wonderful.

Anger

Parents can be angry at their child, themselves, their family, God, outside people who don't understand – and the list goes on.

Eleanor
"I am so overwhelmed with anger, disbelief, rage, betrayal, confusion and profound sadness. I am ashamed to admit my huge disappointment in my daughter. I don't understand how she can dress like a girl, wear make-up, paint her nails, wear earrings, and very much act like a girl and then tell me "When I graduate college, I want to be taking testosterone and making changes to my body and begin living as the male I am." My spirit has been crushed a thousand times. I love her, and I despise her at the same time. I don't want to feel this way at all. I want to learn how to love her no matter who she is. None of my family understands what I am going through. I feel so alone. So sad, so alone and so angry."

Gregory
"Our 47-year-old son just told me he was going to transition and begin living as a woman full-time. We have always been close, but I didn't expect anything like this. He lives on the other side of the country and we only see each other once or twice a year. We have a family wedding in three months. I am mortified to think he will show up at the wedding looking

like a female. He sounds like he is looking forward to attending. I don't think I can handle that. He told me he is beginning to tell people, and that I could discuss his transition with anyone or tell anyone I want. Is he kidding? I'm so angry. I don't want to tell anyone! It's not my job. How could he be so insensitive to my feelings or to the bride and grooms' feelings? I don't want to go to the wedding if he is going to be there."

Anger can present in many ways. It can be expressed as sadness panic, hurt or loneliness. It can seem endless. Underneath anger is pain. Grief is feeling lost at sea. Anger gives an anchor, a temporary structure to the nothing-ness of loss and depression. Anger feels better than nothing. Anger means having your feelings and feelings are energy. It can be a warning sign that that points to boundaries you need to set. Anger can also make you feel like you're going crazy. It can make a liar out of you. You say you're doing fine and, yet your heart feels shattered. You feel people want you to say you're OK because we live in a culture that doesn't know how to grieve. We live in a society that wants us to get back to normal as soon as possible, to keep moving and get on with your life.

Tracy
"My son is 30-years-old and told me three months ago that he was going to transition. My husband has always

been the passive parent. I have made most the decisions. I have been the one the kids come to for almost everything. Now, he is being more supportive that I am. He says that all that matters is that our son is happy. I am so angry at both of them. Can't they see that this is killing me? No, they see me as the problem and the reason why this family is in disarray."

<u>Cynthia</u>
"All I ever wanted was to be a mother to a daughter. I waited until I was 38 and then had in vitro (fertilization) to have her. It took over a year. When I had her, she was everything I had envisioned since I was a young girl. She is 23 now and having her has been the best thing I ever did. She has always come first, and I have loved every minute of being her parent. But now, she wants to change everything. She told me she wants to be a boy and plans on taking testosterone in the next few months. I am so angry at her. She is taking away all I ever wanted. I feel powerless, defeated, and used. To make it worse, she is angry at me for not being happy FOR HER! I don't mean to be selfish, but I keep asking myself, "What about me? Don't I matter?" I've never felt so taken-for-granted and overlooked in my life. I can't believe how little she thinks about my feelings."

You may find yourself angry and blaming others because blame helps us not to feel the pain. You may be angry and blame your child for wanting to make a change, for changing the way they were, or angry that you didn't get more time together with him/her as a boy or girl. You may be angry at yourself for not seeing signs ahead of time and if you did, that you couldn't stop it. Maybe you were the last to know and angry someone else or others were told before you. Angry at God for giving you this challenge. Angry at the transgender community for being there as an influence on your child in ways that you are unaware. Anger at friends who don't understand your loss or anger at the friends who say they want to help but have no idea what you are going through.

Holding on to anger and internalizing it can keep you stuck. It can present in various physical problems such as headaches, ulcers, irritable bowel, eczema, depression and more. To work through anger and let it go, means we need to feel it first. Feel your anger and then look at how you manage it. Taking appropriate ways to let it out can help. Feelings can't be right or wrong. They just are. Try and get to the real reasons you are feeling as you do. If there is more than one reason, try and deal with each event separately. If you have old regrets, remember that regret keeps us stuck in the past and gets in the way of a positive, fulfilling and productive future.

Some parents confess in therapy that they are overwhelmed because they didn't think gender dysphoria or transitioning would be part of the "raising kids" experience that they envisioned. Or, that they feel overwhelmed and unprepared. Often this results in frustration or anger especially when there are sibling and other children's issues to deal with. Some parents feel their anger is endless. Their reaction to hearing this new, may be triggering other times when they felt powerless, felt a deep loss, or felt like something major changed in their life without their consent. If there are unresolved issues of anger or powerlessness in a parent's past, a child's transition could trigger unconscious unresolved issues. Getting professional to get some resolution help could be helpful.

Anger is pain, and it is also a part of healing. It is another indicator of the intensity of your love and commitment to your child. Affirm your power and strength in that you can feel and love. You will come out of this. Your anger will subside. But in the meantime, don't let anyone diminish or criticize the importance of your anger. Not even you. No one likes to be asked to change. Anger temporarily masks the knowing that you can rise above any negative feelings you may have, continue to feel the love for your child, and continue in your hope and excitement for a wonderful future together.

Do I share my feelings of anger, sadness or depression with my child?

As close as you may be to your child, at this point, you are both on different paths. If your child is old enough to perceive your anger or sadness, you may want to initiate a conversation where both of you talk about your feelings. Talking about how transition is affecting both of you, is ideal. For some it may be difficult for both of you to share your experiences. This may be because you are on a path of letting go and dealing with some degree of loss as part of this transition. Your child on the other hand, is most likely living on a path of gain. New identity, new gender expression, new friends, new support. His/her world is usually exciting and full of new experiences, adventure and welcomed change. Although your child may want to be supportive of you, it may or may not feel empathetic to you because they are in a different place. Many children (young or adult) feel sad if their parent is struggling. They may even feel guilty and feel responsible for it. Many want to be supportive. But it is important that the parent and the child get their own support apart from each other. You can still appreciate your child's concern for your feelings, but you want to focus on your parent /child relationship. Continue to spend enjoyable time together and share what you can. Focus on communicating with understanding and mutual respect.

Avoiding Defensive Behaviors

Some things parents do in anger that are not helpful are:

1) They increase the intensity of the attachment

2) They "play ostrich" and pretend it doesn't exist by refusing to face the inevitable.

For example, some parents will attempt to increase the intensity of their attachment to their child by preventing them child from doing anything related to being transgender. They may show their anger by becoming controlling. They may not allow them to attend a transgender support group, have transgender friends, join the LGBT student organization at a high school or college, or express any outward sign with their clothing, hair and accessories that is not congruent with their birth sex. Or, a parent can refuse or ignore the signs and symptoms the child puts in front of them by being passive or passive-aggressive. They can ignore any attempts the child makes to connect and talk with them about their feelings and thoughts. They can overlook obvious changes in appearance, weight, hair color, activities, etc. by not saying anything. They can pretend they are not watching or noticing which often gets interpreted as not caring by the child. Some parents do not feel they are able to accept the changes their child is putting in front of them. Parents need time to learn about what their child is experiencing so they might begin to understand. In the meantime, they may not realize that they inflict shame when they only accept them when they act the way the parent thinks they should act. Some parents feel they can't be positive or supportive because it will "encourage" their child's behavior. Parents need to be aware how important it is to the child to have their support. Teenagers who feel their parents are not supportive have more high-risk behaviors (drugs, alcohol, poor relationship choices, suicide) than those who have support. Parents need to ask themselves what they get out of holding back any love or support and question if they are demonstrating poor parenting behaviors. By being negative, controlling and intimidating, one can get an inflated and immediate sense of superiority. When you blame your child and criticize his/her poor attitude and low self-image, you reinforce a negative self-image. By doing this, you are not taking your part as a parent to support his/her growth and development. By constantly correcting, advising and generally keeping your child dependent, you get to be right and strip him/her of their ability to trust themselves and make their own decisions.

Questions parents need to ask themselves to help get past defensive behaviors:

1) What am I getting out of trying to control the situation?
2) What am I getting out of ignoring the situation?
3) What kind of relationship do I want to have while my child is exploring his gender identity?
4) What can I do to make the relationship/situation better?
5) What do I need to do to take care of myself, so I can feel like a healthy, caring parent?

It is not your child that you want to detach from. It's usually that parents want to detach from the difficult issues they are facing. Maybe it's embarrassment, maybe they feel like they failed as a parent in some way, maybe they feel the future will be empty without their child as they know him/her today. There are issues, but parents still have a healthy child to love and with whom they can have a bright future!

How to Help Yourself Through Anger

1) Know that all your feelings have meaning. You can be angry and still love your child. Take the time you need to be sad or angry and find ways to express it without hurting you or others. Try not to compare your feelings with someone else's. Don't try and speed up your anger. Anger is a part of healing and moving forward. The more you feel it, the sooner it will dissipate. You must feel it to work through it.

2) Have you experienced and overcome any other situation that were unexpected and unwanted initially? How did you manage and cope with that? Reflect on how you overcame that and ask if in the long run it has changed your life for the better.

3) You are not to blame for this. Neither is your spouse, your ex, society, the transgender community, God, etc. Focusing on blaming yourself, others or past events, will always be a waste of your time. Parents sometimes have thoughts such as: "If I spent more time with him/her and was a better parent," "If I didn't get divorced when I did and was more attentive," "If my husband spent more time with him growing up and was more of a role model." None of these concerns cause children to be transgender. This

type of thinking goes nowhere and always results in a dead end. You are not responsible for your child being transgender and therefore have not need to feel guilty about it.

4) This could be a good time to attend a support group. It could be a grief group, general psychotherapy group or ideally, a group for parents of transgender children. When others listen to us or when we share our feelings with others, we heal. Talking and listening helps share the burden, clarifies our thinking and helps us find our own solutions. Meeting others who understand what we are going through, makes us feel less alone. If you feel you are not comfortable in a group of "strangers," remember, no one has to attend a group. People choose to go. It's a way of getting support. So, even though at first you may not know anyone, people who attend groups usually know that everyone there is looking for strength and encouragement. Although they may not know you, in addition to wanting comfort and to feel better themselves, they most likely want you to feel better and get the support you need. There is a common bond. Everyone is coming together with similar issues and goals. Support groups help you find meaningful relationships with people with whom you have things in common.

It's particularly helpful if you are dealing with friends and family member who don't understand or who are not supportive.

5) Be patient with others. Be patient with yourself. Someone may say, "You've got to accept this and move on" or "Don't think you've been sad long enough?" Breathe, stay centered and know that you need and deserve to take whatever amount of time it takes. You will feel better eventually, and if you rush through your feelings, it will take longer to move on.

6) If you tend to struggle with anxiety or depression in general, get professional help if your symptoms are exacerbated. See a doctor, psychiatrist or licensed psychotherapist who specializes in these issues. Get a medical assessment. Do what you can to take charge of your mental and physical health. Consider yoga, meditation, mindfulness, good nutrition, exercise, etc.

7) If you weren't allowed to have anger, sadness or any negative feelings growing up, know that it is OK now. Talk it out, hit a pillow, set the egg timer and yell for five minutes, run, do something physical until you're exhausted. You

can let it out without hurting yourself or anyone else. But let it out.

8) Stay connected to the positive things in your life.

9) Keep doing your routine. If you go to yoga, play piano, watch sports, continue to do those things. It will keep you connected to your own life. Take care of your own activities of daily living.

10) Let your child know you are working through your feelings.

11) Hold on to the things that you love about yourself. Compassion for yourself and keeping an open mind go a long way. You will get through this.

12) Stay connected to what you have and what you are grateful for. Happiness is wanting what you have. Trust that change can brings new awareness and new gifts.

13) Be patient with your spouse if he/she isn't on board. They may not always feel the way they do today. You can still love your spouse even if they feel differently about the transition than you do.

14) You have a child to love who wants you to love them.

Shame and Guilt

Shame and guilt are feelings that result in us feeling poorly about ourselves, but they are different. Guilt is based around action. We may feel guilty because we have done something we regret, or we haven't done something, and we regret that. To overcome guilt, we need to identify what action we need to take to do it differently next time. Parent behaviors don't make a child transgender. It's not about having done something or not done something that makes your child transgender. Therefore, there is nothing to feel guilty about.

Shame is about feeling less than others, but it is not due to an action. Shame is about feeling different and defective just for being who we are.

There is no shame in raising a transgender child or being a parent of a transgender child. In fact, **it's quite the opposite**. Parents of transgender children have the unique opportunity to be proud of themselves and their child. Proud because:

1) They have raised a child who has the courage and strength to be who they are, and who is

willing to go through the journey to make change happen despite adversity.

2) They have the knowledge that not all people see themselves as their birth sex and not all people have a sex and gender that match.

3) They have a deep awareness that life doesn't always give us what we expect and have made the choice to really be there for their child, therefore, parenting with true love, knowing love is bigger and greater than gender.

4) They have the fortitude to be living with an issue that is not main stream and are willing to take that on with grace.

5) They have lived with an issue that has brought them to a place that holds more understanding and compassion for those who are not only transgender or gender variant, but also for anyone living with a condition or situation that is not main-stream.

Most parents feel they could do more to be better parents. Most parents get exhausted and overwhelmed with all the responsibilities associated with doing all they can. Some parents don't try enough. Give yourself credit for being a parent and acknowledge all you have done and given of yourself. Give yourself credit for bringing this child into the world. Give yourself credit for the love you have for your child and the awesome moments, experiences, and challenges you have faced together. Trust that this is another challenge in your parenting path. Trust yourself to make a choice to be the kind of parent you want to be while on this path. You have the choice to be proud of yourself for the way you choose to parent and love your child. Focus on gratitude for all you have, and all you can have in the future.

Chapter 4

The Turning Point: Accepting Reality and Making the Critical Decision

"The toughest part of your child's struggles is finally over. Your child is not dying. Rather, they are finally coming to life. They are the same child you always knew and loved – just happier and free to live as their authentic self."

- Mother of a transman who came out at 26 years old

The Turning Point

There comes a time following grief and emotional feelings, where many parents shift and progress to a new stage. This is where the initial shock and confusion softens and thinking takes over. It is a cognitive state where reason, reality and being rational kick in. I call this stage "The Turning Point." *The turning point happens when parents make the critical decision to fully accept and support their child's transition and do what they can to be a significant and active part of their child's life.* Many parents realize that although it's been a struggle, they do not want to take a back seat to a future they can share together.

A challenge for parents is to ask themselves if they can continue to love their child and accept them for who they are rather than for who the parent may have expected them to be. To get there, parents can begin by demonstrating empathy and imagining what it's like to step in their shoes. Imagine what it would be like to change one's gender, name, and legal information. Imagine all the paperwork and change of documentation involved when a gender change occurs. Changing one's driver's license, diploma, and passport, etc. Often it may mean a change in a career, a divorce, a change of friends and change in social groups. It may mean surgery, painful electrolysis or other uncomfortable medical procedures. It may mean taking medication for the rest of his/her life. It may mean taking a risk of losing everything, just to be able to live and be treated for who they are. Think of what it took for them to get where they are. Think about how important it is that you, the parent, is supportive. Being supportive can look like getting gender-appropriate gifts, treating them in the gender with which he/she self-identifies, using their preferred name, using gender-appropriate pronouns and meeting their friends.

You may see the courage it has taken for your child to come forward with his / her authentic feelings. You can feel happy they have found hope for a positive future as opposed to a troubled and depressing future. You might also want to look at the courage you have had to be where you are in this process.

The more you know the more it will all make sense. It becomes easier when you are open to growth. This looks like learning and feeling new things. Doing this can empower you and give you skills to understand, cope and even embrace what is happening. Finding out facts as well as looking at your fears will strengthen and give you a new awareness. Without this you cannot go forward.

Listen to the part of you that is curious to know more of what is going on in their life and how you can be a part of it. Accepting what we cannot change and letting go of the struggle, helps us find peace and can restore our feeling of control. You may or may not be feeling total acceptance at this point, but you realize you love your child and want to know who they really are and want to be a significant part of their life. This stage is when you are ready to challenge yourself with all that your child wants and needs. You are looking at choices and solutions. The motive here is to restore order to the chaos that was felt previously and go forward learning about gender and transition. Searching for cognitive understanding gives one time to adjust and is another reprieve from pain. There is no reward for suffering. The reward comes when you move into understanding and action.

Getting involved in your child's life and making decisions about it can be empowering and bring you closer to your child. You have good reasons to be involved. If your child is a minor, you may be needed to decide on things like using puberty blockers, helping change their appearance, talking to your child's principal, doctor, dentist, etc. If they are older and feel supported by you, they may be seeking your advice on how to dress, on how they look, on what to tell their children, on what to tell their spouse and other family members. You may find that your willingness to be a part of the change, brings you closer together. You may reach a deeper understanding of how they feel and what you both are going through. They may feel a closer relationship to you, feeling your positive intent and loving support. You may feel happier being involved as a parent.

9 Reasons Why Parents Choose to Accept Reality and Move Forward

1) It's not a stage and it's permanent.
2) Your child is much happier.

3) You miss the happy and fun times you had with your child since most of your energy has been used to cope and survive.
4) You are tired of being detached and resistant.
5) You feel bad that you have not tried enough to understand or be a part of their child's life.
6) You know your child is going to transition whether you are accepting or not and you don't want to lose them or miss a future with them.
7) You want a deeper connection with your child and are ready to learn how to do that.
8) You want to replace fear with facts and are willing to learn about gender issues and make adjustments that support your child's transition.
9) You feel that you can and will survive.

Ask yourself:

1) Is there anything that needs to change before you can fully support your child?

2) What motivates you to accept your child's transition?

3) What do you need to do to take care of yourself through this process?

4) Can you begin to imagine what it will look like to have a good relationship and positive future

between you and your child after they are
completely transitioned?

The turning point is when you are ready to move
forward. It means that you are open to the future and
what it will bring for both you and your child. It also
means you will be able to love them for who they are,
and hopefully, be a significant part of their life. If you
choose not to, you will most likely not fully enjoy the
benefits of an open and trusting relationship, since
they may hide parts of themselves from you feeling
your detachment or disapproval.

It's Not a Stage and It's Permanent

You have seen your child ecstatic for some time
now. There have been plenty of signs, via their
appearance, friends, activities and verbalizations.
The changes parents see in their children, often
helps them to realize that this is permanent. Parents
don't want to fight anymore. They want the struggle to
be over and the conflict to end. Some realize they do
not want to be detached anymore. They see that denial,
anger and depression are not serving them. They know
it's real and permanent and are ready to accept and be
a part of it. Being a part of it may look like learning
about gender, learning about your child or getting
involved in how you can be a positive part of their
life. Transition takes patience, time, money, and is

not easy. Your child has a lot to deal with. If you have not been accepting and your child is older, they may need time to trust you. When realizing its permanent, many parents make a deeper commitment to themselves to learn all they can, communicate more, and take a more active role.

You See Your Child Much Happier

You see your child happier than ever. It may initially feel bitter-sweet since their happiness is when they are expressing their new gender identity, and this may still be awkward for you. But isn't a happy child what you always wanted? You know there is a long road ahead, but now you can have an interest in being a part of it and face the issues at hand. This will most likely bring you closer to your child. Your connectedness may also have you feeling better about yourself in general and may reinforce your feelings of being a loving parent.

Sometimes holding on to things gets in the way of letting things work out the way they are meant to be. What if what we worry about the most, all works out for good? What if the problems bothering you worked out for your child, and was in their best interest and at the right time? What if we knew the future was going to be good, and we had an abundance of resources and guidance to handle whatever comes our way? Sometimes we need to let go of ideas and beliefs that sabotage us and cause frustration. Sometimes we need to let go and remember that life doesn't have to be perfect to be wonderful.

We can't control everything. We can't control a child's desire to want to transition. Although some parents are initially resistant to the idea of transition, the results of transition are ironically the very thing they have always wanted for their child. This realization can be a first step towards acceptance.

Loving Your Child

When asked what parents want for their children, the common responses are:

1) I want my children to be happy and free from problems in life.
2) I want them to enjoy life and appreciate the beauty in life.
3) I want them to feel successful and significant as people regardless of what they do.
4) I want them to have positive feelings about themselves and about life.
5) I want them to grow up with good coping skills.

6) I want them to have a strong sense of inner peace that will sustain them through difficult times.
7) I want them to know they can create and are responsible for their lives and have the power to make choices in their best interest.
8) I want them to value themselves and feel purpose in life.
9) I want them to be able to experience love and love in return.
10) I want them to be able to grow and thrive despite inevitable painful experiences that they encounter in life.

All these desires by the parent are obtainable and available to a transgender child. As the parent, you can be a facilitator to make this happen.

Ask yourself:

1) What do I really want for my child during transition?

2) Is there anything getting in the way for me to give my support?

3) What would I personally have to change before I could give my full support?

4) Are your attitudes and behaviors congruent with being the parent you want to be?

5) If I were to support my child and his/her best interest, what would that look like?

6) Where can I get the support I need?

7) What do I need to do to take care of myself?

Replacing Fear with Facts

Learn all you can about definitions and the meaning of sex, gender, gender identity, gender expression, gender-variant, gender non-conforming, gender-fluid, etc. Gender is no longer accepted as a binary, two-option category. Explore to the fullest, what is currently known and understood about gender. Compare this with what you were raised to believe about gender as a child. Learn specifics about hormones, surgery, and details of transition.

If possible, learn all you can about your child. How long they have been struggling? If you thought your child was "different," you may now want to explore if any of their shyness or withdrawal was related to gender dysphoria. You may have the strength to ask questions today without being afraid of the answers.

What does your child want and/or need from you? If they are adults, what do you need from them? Assess what the relationship between you and your child has been like. Have you had the kind of relationship with them that you wanted to have? If not, you may be feeling some regret, wishing you had spent more time together. If that is true, will you consider spending more time with them now? What will change and what won't in your relationship? Can you initiate communication about your relationship? What are his/her expectation? What are yours? This is also a good time to get support and meet other families with gender-variant children or children going through transition if you haven't done that already.

Keep communication as open as possible. Try and be open to learning new ideas and paradigms about gender. You may have been afraid to ask questions prior to this but facing them can overcome irrational and unrealistic fears.

Go online. Find a good support group with other parents going through similar feelings. Find a friend you can trust or get professional support. Remind yourself that you can still be a good parent while working through your feelings.

Ask yourself:

1) What are your fears/concerns at this stage?

2) How do you see your role as mother/father/caretaker now? Do you think that will change? If so, how?

3) What activities do you see your son/daughter doing in the future?

4) Can you envision you and your child enjoying a future together?

5) What do you feel comfortable telling people (friends, family, others) when they ask about you or your child? Can you feel a difference between how you feel now and feelings you had previously?

As one parent said when asked what parents need to know to help them get through their child's transition:

"The best thing I did to help me was to educate myself, find support, and use the internet. I learned to listen more and talk less. In the beginning, I found myself in tearful conversations that usually resulted in someone being hurt. In my earnest quest to understand, accept,

and provide "helpful parenting advice" I found that I asked too many of the "wrong" questions, and made statements that I later learned were received "offensively." Conversations went better once I allowed my adult child to take the lead."

— *Mother of a 32-year-old transwoman*

Maybe this entire experience came into your life to teach you something. Maybe it is about learning you have choices on how to deal with whatever happens to you. It's not always about what happens to us, but how we perceive what happens to us, that matters. How we perceive it, is what we get. We always heal and go forward. We can choose peace and stay in control of ourselves and our life.

Let your curiosity, openness, strength, love for your child and love of your role as a parent guide you. Make sure you have some fun and let yourself enjoy what you can on this path with your child. Do your part to create a joyful and loving future.

Benefits of Acceptance

1) You get to quit struggling with something over which you have no control.

2) You get to learn how to choose peace.

3) You get to survive a time of sadness. You can readjust and get involved. You can be resilient.

4) You get to see your child alive and to see them bloom. You get to see them happier and more open about who they are than you have ever seen before. You develop an appreciation and respect for their strength. You also get to see them live out the values that you have taught them.

5) In time, you may find that your role in their new life has brought opportunities for you.

6) You get to see that you matter and are important. You have an opportunity to feel stronger, smarter and richer in life experience.

7) You get the gift of expanding your comfort zone and seeing there are other ways to look at gender than the one you grew up with. You can be more educated and empathetic to the world of those who are not born into a binary-gender world.

8) Your focus changes from loss to a life that can be fully lived.

9) You can heal and embrace the future with hope, openness and a positive attitude for a future with happiness and fulfillment.

10) You get to live with peace.

Helpful Tips to Take Care of You

Know that anyone can change if they want to.

Be open to a new relationship with your child and remind yourself that what you want is for them to live a healthy and happy life.

Have faith in the process.

You probably know more than you think you do and you will likely start seeing yourself as stronger than you thought possible.

Appreciate your good parenting skills as evidenced by noticing what is important and necessary for your child and what is important and necessary for you.

Appreciate your ability to take care of yourself by accepting reality and deciding to move on and enjoy your life.

Chapter 5

Family Issues

"When anyone in a family transitions their loved one's transition as well."

When Your Spouse Does Not Feel the Same as You

N ot all spouses deal with their feelings regarding transition at the same time or in the same way. Anger, frustration and depression are often exacerbated when your spouse feels differently from you or is not empathetic to your feelings. Just when you feel you need support, you may experience loneliness and feel that you are taking this on all by yourself. Some spouses don't know what to do, so they respond by avoiding or ignoring the issue. They may use work or another responsibility as an excuse. They may not be equipped to deal with their feelings regarding the impact their child will have on them. Some parents are not supportive because they feel that would be "encouraging them" (the child) to be transgender. Some parents overact, take it personally or fall apart not knowing what to do. If your spouse, does not feel the same as you, you may want to tell them that this is something you'd like to share and experience together. Saying, "I need you to be there for me" is too vague. It leaves the partner hanging, maybe feeling guilty and pressured to do something but with no understanding or idea of what to do. It's always good to ask for what you need. Make it positive, specific and measurable. "I'd like to talk about Mark and his transition with you. How about Saturday morning? We can go out for breakfast at about 10. Does this work for you?" Or "I'd like to have some time alone with you this week, for us to talk about Mark's transition. What time works for you?" Specifying that you want to do this together, does two things. It is a request for connection and at the same time, a way to offer support. If your partner is not willing to connect, find someone else you trust to share your feelings and concerns.

Whether parents are supportive or not, it's important the child is allowed to talk about their feelings. If they can't talk about who they are, they will feel something is wrong with them in your eyes and their feelings will turn to shame. Shame is feeling "less than" and that "there is something wrong with me." No one can feel good about themselves or feel safe if they have to hide and lie

about who they are, especially in their own home or
with someone they love.

When Your Spouse Knew and Didn't Tell You

Another problem for some parents, is when one
parent knows, and the other doesn't. Children who
feel closer to one parent, often confide in that parent
and ask that they not tell the other. Children often
confide in the parent they feel will be the most
understanding and supportive. It may be hard for
the parent who has the information, to hold on to it,
particularly if the child told him/her privately, and
asked them not to tell. This parent might feel "in the
middle," wanting to respect the child's request, but
wanting to also tell the spouse. The parent who
finds out later may be hurt and angry for being "the
last to know." This could also create a trust issue
between the parents. When to tell the other parent is
different in each situation. Ideally, it is best for both
parents to know at the same time, but it doesn't
always work this way. If you are the parent who
was told first, and you feel uncomfortable keeping
this from your spouse, let your child know how you
feel. Let them know you are uncomfortable and
why you feel it may be time to tell your spouse,

explaining the focus is on going forward together.
Ask if they are ready to tell the other spouse and
discuss their reasons calmly if they are not. Your
child may take your thoughts seriously and your
discussion may facilitate movement towards telling
your spouse, particularly if you say you are
uncomfortable holding a secret. If not, it at least can
keep both of you connected, having communicated
how each other feels. You may be the parent who is
angry at your child for telling the other parent or
another family member before you. No one likes to
be the last to know. You can tell them how you feel
and ask why they made the choice they did, if you
are unclear. Let them know how you feel, and if
they would be more open with you in the future.
Then, focus on going forward.

Sibling Grief

Sibling grief refers to the grief siblings feel when
they are grieving the relationship they had with a
brother or sister who is transitioning. This does not
mean they are not accepting. Even when siblings
are supportive, they can experience loss of the
relationship they had before. The grief is about the
ending of one chapter and about what you will not
experience together because of the change. If you
imagined your younger sister being the maid of

honor at your wedding, and now she is transitioning, you may grieve the ideas and dreams of how you thought it was going to be. As a parent, the age of the sibling and your present relationship with them, will give you some guidelines as to what to say and how much to step in. For a six-year-old sibling who has a 14-year-old brother who is transitioning, it will be confusing that she will now have an older sister. Your job would be to educate and show support for both. Very young children, under 5 are usually accepting since they are focused more on the connection, not the gender. If the child is a 33-year-old with two siblings ages 27 and 31, you may want to talk to each sibling separately and find out what their feelings are. If all are supportive and you have a good relationship with them, you may want to talk about how all of you can help as a family. If there is discord by adult siblings, you need to let them have their own feelings. You can influence them to be supportive, but you can't rush them or manipulate them to feel something they don't.

Seeing discord and rivalry among siblings can be hurtful to parents. You can stay connected and let them know you are always open to discussion. You can have family meetings to discuss how transition is affecting each sibling. You can suggest professional counseling if you see one of your children struggling. If you or your adult child have a distant relationship with a sibling or step-sibling, you are not responsible to find them and tell them. It will be up to the adult transitioning to tell who they choose.

Karen and Margaret

Karen and her twin sister Margaret are 22 years-old. They attended private girls camp every summer from when they were five years old to 18. They grew up doing everything together and were very close although they didn't always think alike or agree. They were thrilled to be chosen to work as counselors at their summer camp there after they graduated high school. Now, four years later, Karen found out that her sister is in process of transitioning to living full-time as male. Karen is grieving that she no longer will have a sister. She is angry at her sister for "abandoning" her. Karen becomes overwhelmed with rage when she thinks about going back to camp and others asking her "Where's your sister?" She is thinking of quitting to avoid having others confront her and angry at her sister for what she feels is "putting her in this position" since she doesn't want to leave. She is angry with herself, for not feeling supportive of her sister's transition. She claims she loves her sister but is in deep grief. She claims she can't imagine losing her twin sister and their connection. She can't imagine having a twin brother. She feels abandoned and that she has lost the most important relationship in her life.

Because a sibling is "close," they may have a hard time adjusting. Or, because they are "close," they adjust quickly, giving support and being there from the beginning. They may embrace the news "with open arms" being as willing to help as they can. Some siblings may be the first to know. Others may be angry because they weren't. Siblings may not all be accepting or reach levels of acceptance at the same time. Siblings are notorious for quickly adjusting to the new name change but get stuck on changing the pronouns.

As a parent, how do you handle this? Of course, it's easier when you have an open and loving attitude. Listen to the other siblings. Let them vent their feelings. Validate their concerns. Young ones may be looking to you to set the stage of how they "should" act. Older siblings who are not accepting may need support by you or a professional to help them.

Family Conflicts

Shirley
Shirley, a 27-year-old biological female, dated women exclusively in high school and throughout her first two years of college. Although she never introduced her female partners to her parents. Both parents suspected she was lesbian. Shirley secretly had symptoms of gender dysphoria throughout her life. During her second year at college, she discovered she was transgender. By the time she graduated college, she changed her name legally to Steve and now lives full-time as a male. Steve came out to his parents prior to having his name legally changed. His parents were not shocked with Steve's decision, yet, after a year, they find themselves occasionally saying "she" instead of "he" when referring to Steve. After a year, they say they are sometimes still in disbelief that they have a son.

Maura
Maura is a 60-year-old accountant who loves and spends a great deal of time with her 12 and 14-year-old granddaughters. Recently, Maura's 35-year-old daughter, told Maura, that she was transgender. Maura was shocked and thought that transitioning was only for people who had no children. Her initial reaction was that of anger towards her daughter, thinking she was being "selfish" and "unfair" to her granddaughters. She did not feel she could be supportive of her daughter's transition, particularly in front of her grandchildren. Much to her surprise, her granddaughters

were supportive of their mother, and as a result, Maura now feels there is a wedge between herself and her granddaughters. She came to therapy to process her anger with her daughter for "creating a situation where my grandchildren and I are at odds."

Readjusting Roles

Transition means change and with that comes readjusting your role as a parent. Look at your role as mother, father, step-mother, step-father, primary caregiver. What does that look like now? What does that look like during and after transition? As a dad, can you have "guy night" with your newly transitioned son? Or, "father-daughter" night with your newly transitioned daughter? As a mom, can you also make time to get to know your child in their new gender identity? Quality time with your children can give you time to create and establish realistic expectations for your relationship. Will you be doing the same things you did before for fun? Or, will it be different? Will anything stay the same?

If your son always purchased and delivered the Christmas tree for the family the week before Christmas, will he continue to want to do that as a woman? If you are wondering if your child will continue certain behaviors, roles, activities after they have transitioned, ask them. Don't stress. They will tell you what they are comfortable with and what they aren't. You can also tell them what you are comfortable with and what you aren't.

Being together will give you time to communicate and decide together what experiences will change, what will remain the same. Keep the focus on enjoying your time together.

Ask yourself:

1) What specific activities will change?

2) What activities that you enjoyed doing together will stay the same?

3) What do you see your relationship will be like with your child?

4) How will you feel about parenting now?

5) Can you have fun with it?

6) What were the roles your child filled?

7) What roles will they fill now?

8) What were the roles you filled for your child?

9) What roles will you fill now?

Resources

The World Professional Association of Transgender Health Organization, (WPATH) at www.WPATH.org, sets standards of care for people who want to transition. WPATH is a world-wide organization that provides clinical guidance for health professionals to assist transgender and various gender nonconforming people with safe and effective pathways to achieving lasting personal comfort with their true selves. They promote overall health, psychological well-being and self-fulfillment. You can go to their web site to find the latest information on transgender health as well as find therapists in your area.

Parents and Friends of Lesbians and Gays (PFLAG) at www.PFLAG.org, also provides information and support. PFLAG is a national organization for friends and family members of LGBT (lesbian, gay, bi-sexual and transgender) people. They provide educational meetings, support groups and are active with community outreach. They are located throughout the country. Many have transgender family support groups. You can go on line to find PFLAG meetings and LGBT centers in your community. There is loving help and kind support out there to find out all you want to know. Meetings provide a great way to develop relationships with others who may have similar situations and experiences.

There are a multitude of resources who offer education, support and community for parents and families on the internet. There is also You Tube, Amazon books on gender related issues, national support groups, and local LGBT support groups in your area. By reaching out you may feel like you are taking back some control of your life. Reaching out is a good way to take care of you. Put only positive people around you. People you respect and appreciate, who understand and support you.

Guidelines for Parents

1) Keep your home a safe and secure place for you, your child and your family. Make it a place where you can share your feelings and experiences together. If you are all living together, it might look like having family meetings. These can be scheduled ahead of time. They can also be scheduled in advance and held regularly. This would give everyone a framework for knowing the talks are on-going. For example, a weekly meeting might give some members a time to look forward to. The idea is that everyone is encouraged to be a part of the

discussion and everyone's input is valued. The meetings could include personal feelings, comments from others, family concerns and any gender related issue. It may include experiences other siblings are having at school, with friends or others regarding their sibling's transition. The purpose would be to give support and strength to all family members and deal with each other's situations or issues of concern.

2) Be as honest and genuine as you can with your feelings to yourself, your family, and those you trust with your feelings. When you experience a variety of appropriate feelings in front of your children, you are letting them know that feelings are healthy. When they see you manage and cope with your feelings, you model that working through feelings is a healthy part of coping and coming to terms with issues. If a family member senses you are being genuine about how you feel, they too will often respond in a more genuine manner.

3) Let others know that you want the best for your child and that requires kindness, support and respect from others. You can't change anyone but yourself, but you can have boundaries. This means you can let others know which behaviors

work for you, and which behaviors don't. You can let them know that any type of shaming, bullying or disrespect to your child is not OK. You can also ask that they have kind and supportive words to others when discussing your family with others when you are not there.

4) Do not shame your child when they are in process of experiencing living in the other gender. This means, don't put down their clothing, their physical appearance, their new friends or their new behaviors. Don't ask them to not be who they are. They need to find out how they can best fit in with their new expression of themselves. They may need your support while trying to identify what works for them.

5) Don't use religion to shame or control your child. You don't want to take away the importance of having spirituality or religion in their life. For some, this is a major source of strength, stability, comfort, hope and peace. Taking this away could be damaging to their sense of self and their soul.

6) Make it a point to discuss how your child's new gender may change his/her roles in the family. Discuss the new gender and what this new role

might look like. Also, find out if there anything your child would like from the family to validate acceptance and love in this new role. For example: calling him/her by a different name, using different pronouns, having different expectations.

7) Develop a support system of people who can be there for you. Rely on therapists and other professionals for help when necessary for you or your child.

Chapter 6

Telling others. What do you say?

Fear of Judgment

P arents worry about how others will react to the
news and what others will think of them for
having a transgender child. You didn't make your
child transgender. And even if it were possible, it's
nothing to be ashamed of. You can overcome fear of
judgement by reminding yourself that your child is
precious and perfect just the way he/she is. You
brought this soul into the world to live a unique
path. You as the parent, have a front row ticket to
the best show on earth. Now you get to live it with
all its peaks and valleys. What a journey! And you
are an important part of that journey. You want to
get beyond the "Maybe it wouldn't have happened
if I didn't get divorced and he had more time to
spend with a male role model" or "I should have
spent more time with her teaching her how to be
feminine," or "What will my family think of me
now?" or "What will my friends think about me as a
mother/father?"

There is no fault and no one to blame. Would you feel others would judge you if your child were left-handed? That is not main-stream either. Is it rational to look for someone to blame or to doubt yourself? No. Life is a tapestry. Gender is fluid. Parents are here to love and encourage. Children of all ages teach their parents about life.

It's likely that as time goes by and people find out, you will quickly get to know who is on your side and who isn't. True friends will be there with you. You can trust them with your deepest thoughts and concerns. You know who will be there. Those with doubts, confusion and who appear rejecting, may likely fade from your life with time. Not everyone's initial reaction is their true reaction. Some people need time to process their feelings. You are not responsible for their reaction. If they continue to feel judgmental or unaccepting, you can detach. You don't want to stand up for anything or anyone who does not support you. Although rejection is painful, there is plenty of love and support when you reach out and look for it. You can't change anyone but yourself. Detach with love from those who aren't supportive. Connect with love to those who are.

What to Say

Telling our truth and being who we are takes risk. There comes a time in life when we become willing to liberate ourselves and stop allowing ourselves to be controlled by others and their expectations of us. If we lose people by being who we are, it may never have been healthy to have that relationship anyway. When we are authentic, we have more intimacy and relationships that work.

Telling anyone that you have a transgender child can be smooth or challenging. For some, it may feel like taking a risk. You may have different feelings depending on who you are telling. In general, it will be as comfortable for you as you are with the situation. It will be much easier and smoother if you know what to say and are comfortable saying it. The more prepared you are, the less challenging it will be.

Questions to prepare for challenging reactions

Whether it be a family member, sibling, friend, or acquaintance, ask yourself these three questions regarding their reaction:

1) What is possible?
2) What is predictable?
3) What is fantasy?

Writing the answers down or practicing this ahead of time with a spouse or trusted friend, can make it much easier. The more prepared you are, the easier things will be. You are only responsible for your half of the conversation. Your position is to get the information out. You are not responsible for another's reaction. By getting the information out, you have done your part. Say what you need to say and let it go. You need to be able to set boundaries if necessary. You cannot set a boundary and be responsible for the other person's feelings at the same time. So, think about it, write down your answers to the three questions ahead of time, and practice each response with someone you trust. Practicing in advance makes you more prepared when you run into people who catch you off guard. You can be more comfortable and at ease when you are prepared and know what you are going to say. Again, know you are responsible for what you say only, not their reaction. When telling someone for the first time who has had no idea of what is going on, you might want to tell them and then suggest they get back to you in a couple of weeks if they have any questions. This will give them time to process.

Another suggestion, for those you don't see on a regular basis is to send them a letter or message them in the way you think is most appropriate for that relationship. Tell them there are changes happening in your family. If your child looks differently than the last time they were seen by the person you are writing, you may also send a picture of your child or a family photo with your child looking as they are now. This gives people time to process and think. You can end your message with, I'll get back to you in a couple of weeks to see if you have any questions. Or, feel free to call me in a couple of weeks if you have any questions.

Many people start out with something like, "There has been a change in our family and because you're important to us, I'd like to tell you about it." Then you can go on to say that your child has been identified as having a medical condition called gender dysphoria, and as a result, they are going to look and live differently than they did in the past. Your child may be going through a social transition, medical transition or just living with an altered gender expression. Not all people with gender issues make a full transition. So, you would need to share information specific to your situation. If your child is transitioning, you can then say how positive it has been for your child to have this realization, and how committed you are to be loving your child, and that you are supporting them. Always end your discussion with what you want from them. You may end with something like, "we just want you to know, and after you think about it, we hope you will feel as supportive as we are," or "When you see Tom again, "he" would like you to call him by his new name, Tina, and use the correct pronouns that correspond with being female. (she, her, hers).

If the family is not feeling that supportive and it is someone you trust, you can say that also. The idea is for you to share information, be comfortable, and not to say more than you want with each specific person. If someone asks you a question that is inappropriate or that you don't want to answer, you can politely and quietly say, "I need time to think about that, let me get back with you," or "I don't know if (your child) feels I should discuss more at this point, so I'd rather not answer that at this time." Limiting your answer is not mean or curt, it is establishing a boundary. People who respect you and your family will understand.

If someone asks what they can do to help, let them know. You may ask for them to call you occasionally to talk, you may ask them to speak kindly of you and child when others bring it up, you may ask someone you trust to go to a support group with you. Do whatever you feel will help you. Be mindful of the love in the offering to help. Notice and be grateful for the support others give you.

It is likely that your child, depending on their age, will have already "come out" to friends, family members and others already. You may want to have a talk with them to see who already knows and discuss who is going to tell whom.

It can be very difficult when your child comes out later in life, after their 30's, when you have a lifetime of friends from several walks of life who knew your family unit as it was for many years. Some will accept it readily and some won't, which can create awkward family and social situations, particularly if you are not prepared. If you have a spouse or significant other, talk with them about who to tell and when. If your child is an adult, discuss with them how they want others including immediate family, extended family, and friends to know. Some adult children want their parents to be involved in the telling. Others take full responsibility and "come out" to all by themselves. Most people come out to immediate family and their closest people face to face. Other significant people are often told via letter. There is no right or wrong, people need to do it the way they feel most comfortable. How much you tell is also determined by how close you are to the person being told. Close people may get more information. More distant people usually are told the basics.

Family Members

There is no perfect way to deal with family members. We all need to choose what works for us. We can be grateful for those who understand and are supportive and we can set boundaries with those who are not. We can give people time to get educated on gender issues and transition. Hopefully, the love they feel for your child will inspire them do what they need to do to be supportive. Having supportive family members who are loving and accepting, can be of extreme importance to someone who is transitioning. Initially, all family members may not be supportive at the same time. Some come around later. You can't force someone to be accepting. Most family members need time to process their feelings.

Belinda
Belinda is a 32-year-old transwoman. Her father left her mother and five sisters when she was 14 years old. She was the oldest and stepped up to take care of all of them. Eventually, she moved to another state and earned her medical degree. It took her mother and sisters a couple of years to accept Belinda. They liked her being the "male" in the family. Although her mother and sisters are accepting, her grandmother who lives with her mother is not. When Belinda goes "home" to visit, her grandmother

shames her and calls her by her "dead" (old male) name. This causes friction between her mother and grandmother.

You can love a family member who does not think the same way you do. You can love them and still do what you think is right. Pleasing someone else at your expense is called codependency. If you have to lose yourself, to have a relationship with someone else, the relationship is not healthy. If someone tries to tell you that if you don't think or act like them, that you don't really love them, you need to beware. That is their way of manipulating you. They either want to see if they have control over you to make you change your mind, or they are looking for a reason to have a power struggle.

Healthy people want you to do what you feel is best for you. The definition of maturity is to know your values and to be able stand up for them. This goes for dealing with family members too. Healthy people accept differences. In a healthy relationship, you don't have to think alike to get along, but you do need to *respect the differences*. Boundaries are limits that separate one thing from another. We need to keep healthy boundaries with family member who are not supportive. It is fine to detach with love from a family member or anyone who does not respect your decision to live a healthy life and do what is best for your family. This is true whether you have a child who is transitioning or not. It is especially true if your child is transitioning and they are refusing to try and understand the situation. If someone is toxic in your family and make things worse, you may want to detach significantly. Don't try and convince someone toxic to be rational. Being around toxic people is like watering a dead plant. This goes for family members too.

In general, if a friend or family member tells you they are uncomfortable with the news, it's OK to acknowledge that initially, you may have been uncomfortable too. Tell them you understand it may take time. If it takes more time than you are comfortable with, you might want to distance yourself. Depending on the age of the child and the situation, you can also request, when appropriate, that they do not share their negative feelings with your child. You may tell them this could negatively affect your child's progress.

If you child is a minor, writing or calling family members is appropriate. If you see them regularly, you can talk face-to-face. Let them know about your child's gender issues. If you are supportive you can say so. You can answer their questions and ask them not to say anything that might send a message of unacceptance. You can let them know what you expect of them in terms of their behavior. Remind them that your child is more than his/her gender. If they are uncomfortable, let them know what your child's interests are, so they will have safe topics to discuss. If they are older, they can talk with their extended family members themselves. They can write them a letter, tell them they are transgender and say they will get back to them to answer any questions they may have. Often, family members will connect once they receive the letter, often to give support.

The more you learn to speak with acceptance and support, the easier it will be for others to follow your lead. You have nothing to apologize or be ashamed about. It's your job to take care of your child, yourself and your family. Speak to others with support of your child. For example, you can say, "Isn't it great my child is not afraid to be himself/herself."

Choose the path that is right for you and your child. Your goal is to be able for you and your child to take care of yourself, love yourself and live a healthy life despite what family members do or don't do. You can also tell family members how important it is or that you would appreciate that you and your family have their support.

Siblings

Gender diversity can create issues for everyone.
Parents may bond with their children whose gender
matches their sex at birth (cis) more than gender-
variant or trans children, because of society's
discomfort with gender diversity. Or, parents may
focus on the needs of the gender-variant or trans
child, sensing they need more attention and overlook
the sibling(s).

In general, young children are creative and it's
common for them to see fantasy in movies, cartoons,
videos and games. Cat Woman and Spiderman jump
across buildings, animals talk, the planets and the
trees and stars can sing. They hear stories and see
movies where spells are put on animals and people
which makes them change into something else.
Middle school and high school kids see men in rock
bands wear make-up, and what looks like girl's
accessories and clothing. They see girls with
masculine tattoos, androgynous anime art, and male
ballet and flamenco dancers in feminine costumes.
They also see movies where men dress up like women.
Because of social media and because most kids have
access to technology, they are exposed to gender
being more fluid and much less binary than the
generation before them. It may not be a big stretch

for some to imagine a man transform to a woman or vice versa.

Although exposed to gender fluidity, some siblings may not be so accepting of a brother or sister transitioning. A transitioning sibling affects them directly, and personally. It may even embarrass them, especially if they are at an age where "fitting in" is paramount. This is particularly true of children in middle school. Siblings have various reactions to their brother or sister changing. If it is traumatic for them, as a parent you can intervene to ask questions and support them. Children will often take on the feelings of the parents. If the parent is negatively affected, or if the child is asked to guard it as a family secret, the child may take on a negative attitude. If it comes across as bad or a secret, there will likely be shame transferred to the sibling.

Reactions of siblings can range from: 1) Acting out to gain attention and be noticed if they feel left out; 2) retreating and withdrawing; 3) being jealous of the attention their sibling is getting, and as a result, tease or bully the sibling; 4) they may be defending their transgender sibling out of protection, love or obligation. Parents need to make a point to talk about gender objectively and as it relates to all

143

people. Some siblings may need professional support. Professional help can be helpful and supportive to you as well, so you do not have to take it all on yourself. Family counseling may also be helpful.

Handling Negative Reactions

We never have to prove to others that we, or our child in this case, are good enough. Proving how good we are, or how right we are can all be an indication that we are trying to control someone. Trying excessively to make a point with another may mean that we are struggling to believe it ourselves. Focus on accepting your child and making your life work, rather than trying to push people to be accepting. Yet, telling people and dealing with their reaction is part of the process. It's very important you do not get stuck in a situation that is overly uncomfortable for you. Should someone ask you a question that you feel is too personal or inappropriate, you do not have to answer. Stay poised and in control. Redirect the question with a positive response if possible. The important thing is to not be put on the spot! Have boundaries. Having boundaries means teaching people how to treat you. It means letting people know that "this works for me and this doesn't." How you talk about your child and your family and how you are doing, will let people know how you feel. They will also get a feel for what responses are OK with you and which ones aren't. If they are not perceptive or are aggressive and it gets difficult, try and be calm. Breathe. Stay grounded. Think about your support system where you get empathy and compassion. Don't stay too long in a conversation that is not going anywhere. Don't stay engaged with people who are toxic. Incorporate the following, or any responses that are comfortable for you. You may want to write down and review what responses you are comfortable with ahead of time. This way you will be more prepared when talking to others.

Negative Comments

"Oh my God, you must be devastated!"

"Is he going to have surgery?"

"What will you tell people at church?"

"I feel so sorry for you" "You much be horribly embarrassed."

"That's just not right or natural, what are you going to do about it?"

Responses

"Yes, I was a shocked at first, but with all I've learned about gender lately, I'm developing a lot of compassion for the many people who struggle with their gender issues. I had no idea how prevalent these issues are."

"All I want is for _____ (my child) to have a full life being who they truly are."

"Surgery is not what we are dealing with at this time. We are taking it one day at a time."

"I'm sure that many people are going to find out, even those we don't tell. I hope if it comes back to you, I will have your support in saying something kind".

"I'm telling you because you are important to me and I hope _____ (child's name) and I have your support."

"This has challenged all of us, but I expect it will bring our family even closer in many ways."

"I'm loving seeing _____(name) so happy with his/her discovery of his/ her true self."

"I'm not embarrassed at all. Quite the opposite. I am so proud of _____ (child's name), for having the strength and courage to come forward and take a stand about who he/ she is."

"I know some people feel it's may not be "right" or "natural." I'm not trying to change anyone's opinion. I'm just doing what is right for me, _____ (child's name) and our family".

"I don't feel I know you well enough to go into more personal details at this time."

"Yes, there are many issues to deal with and we are taking it one day at a time."

Also, if you don't want to answer, you can respond, "I'll have to think about that and get back to you".

Confrontations are best when the person confronting ends with a request. If you are talking with someone and you know what you would like from them, ask.

"I would like it if you could be positive and supportive of me and _____ (child's name) at_____ (i.e., work, church, the synagogue, the family reunion, with the neighbors, etc.)."

You can't always protect your child from unsupportive people. It may be good for older children to know who is not supportive. This way they can make decisions about who is safe and who isn't. If your child is young and struggling and you know the person you are talking to is not supportive or has doubts, you could say: "I would appreciate it if you didn't share any negative feelings you have with _____ (child's name) about this at this time. We are wanting him/her to feel supported and loved through this process."

Cultural, Racial and Religious Influences

Sometimes people have cultural, racial or religious beliefs that influence acceptance or lack of support for transitioning. You may even get some rigid feedback that transition is not "right" either in the eyes of God or as a part of the culture. To be healthy, strive for love in relationships, not superiority. Parents learn that it's important to do what is right for them and their child. What others do, or think is their business. You don't need to allow anyone to shame or bully you into religious or cultural beliefs that don't support you or your child. Take the good, from your religion, race or culture. Discover and develop your own path that works for you spiritually. Give thanks for a healthy child, made perfect, and honor the divinity that manifested this miracle for you.

Try and be patient with those who don't understand or want to understand how important their love and support would mean to you. Particularly if you have been a part of a group where you felt love and have been accepted. It will be up to you to create boundaries with those people and places that are not safe. Ask yourself if there are any benefits in standing up for someone or something that does not support you.

James

James was the oldest child of six children. His father died when he was 9 and he helped his mother raise his younger siblings. He grew up in the ghetto of a large city where being African-American meant living with plenty of bullying and discrimination. James was exceptionally bright and went on to be a successful lawyer and business owner. Now, he lives in another large city where he feels safe and respected both professionally and personally and his life is more pleasant and stable than it was growing up. He came to therapy saying he had symptoms of gender dysphoria all his life but could never display them since he didn't want to add to the bullying and discrimination he was already experiencing. He fears he will return to being discriminated against if he comes out as transgender. He also lives with a fear his family will reject him. He lives in an increasing, constant state of distress. Except for therapy, he keeps his feelings to himself and admitted he sometimes feels suicidal.

James' experience of growing up with bullying because he was African-American adds to his fear/shame when thinking about coming out. His desire to avoid making himself a target to more bullying and discrimination as a transwoman, has caused him to put off his desire to move forward with a transition. His feelings of being stuck, underline his suicidal thoughts. Had his situation been different, he might be more willing to go forward.

<u>Monica</u>
Monica is a 27-year-old woman who was raised in a fundamental Christian church and has worshipped there all her life. The gender dysphoria she has experienced since

childhood has become harder to ignore in the last year. Six months ago, she came out to the senior minister of the church, saying she was transgender and going to make a transition. At first, many parishioners came to her home, saying why she should not do this. After about three months, people stopped coming to her home, she was notified she is no longer welcome to worship there and was dropped as a member.

Monica's rejection by the church was an additional stress she had when making her transition. Parents who are aware that there can be added stress for a child due to cultural, racial or religious influences are in a better position to support their child. It also gives parents an appreciation of themselves for their insight, awareness and empathy.

Holidays, Religious Rituals and Social Situations

Rachel
Rachel, who is almost 13 years old, has been raised Jewish and has attended Hebrew school for the last three years. She has been studying Hebrew to prepare for her Bat Mitzvah. (a Jewish coming-of-age ritual for girls). She "came out" to her parents three years ago saying she was a boy. The family is accepting but is struggling now since Rachel refuses to have a Bat Mitzvah and wants a Bar Mitzvah (the coming-

of-age ritual for boys). This ceremony is very important to her family and Rachel is giving them a hard time. The Rabbi at the synagogue has been informed and is not supportive of "her" having a Bar Mitzvah with the boys. Her parents are conflicted about what to do and wondering what they will say to their friends at the synagogue or to those who haven't see her for a while, when they ask about her Bat Mitzvah.

Dan

Dan recently graduated from college. One evening, he and his parents went to dinner at the country club where they have been members for 15 years. Their family was well known to many other members. Dan had made a full transition his senior year at college but hadn't told anyone in his home town. He was now living full-time as Diane. While Diane, her parents and two sisters were seated having dinner at the club, an old friend walked over to the table to greet them. The friend looked around at everyone at the table (including Diane) and then asked, "Where's Dan?" Dan and his parents were unprepared as to how to respond.

It's important to be pro-active and as prepared as you can when you are about to go into a social situation when your child has transitioned. Some people need to be informed ahead of time if possible. No one wants an uncomfortable situation but it's almost unrealistic to think it won't happen.

Holidays, family reunions and weddings are not a time to "come out." If someone does, it will have shock value and take the focus off the event they are attending. If your child is transitioning and you know there is going to be a family reunion in six months, you might want to consider writing a letter to the close people in your life, telling them of the change way before the event. I suggest sending a picture, so they will have an idea of what your child will look like when they see them. I also suggest that at the end of the letter, you say you will follow up with them in a couple of weeks to see if they have any questions. You could also ask them to contact you if they have any questions. People need time to digest this kind of information, so giving time is important. If you get back with them later, they will have had time to process their feelings and be more prepared to speak with you. By preparing people ahead of time, your child can go to the event and the significant people in your life will be prepared. If your child is not a minor, I suggest they write the letter themselves.

How to Help Yourself

Know that your attitude when discussing your child may be more important than your words and people will always sense if what you're saying is authentic. So, be assertive, have boundaries, keep conversations short with people with whom you feel uncomfortable and be as real as possible. Share as much as you want with those your love. No matter who you talk to, you are not responsible for anyone's reaction or their happiness. You are just responsible to take care of you and your child and your family.

Never be apologetic. Most people have already spent too much time being ashamed, being apologetic, and doubting the unique and brilliant person they are. Others are entitled to their opinion, but so are we. Love and appreciate yourself and don't look to others to get your approval. Sometimes being healthy means walking away, not in weakness but in strength. Sometimes being healthy means to detach with love.

Never be defensive. If you're not sure what to say, don't say anything. When we get defensive we lose our power. Not saying anything can be a choice. It doesn't mean we don't have anything to say. We just realize that with some people, it's just not worth it.

Use conflict as a way of learning coping skills. You can breathe, relax and go with the flow. If someone doesn't think the way you do, no matter how important they are to you, you don't have to panic or become desperate. You won't drown. Everyone has their own path. Stay focused and centered on yours. You don't have to miss the fun or not enjoy life because of someone else's opinion.

Throughout this time of telling others, make sure you have an inner circle of support. Include specific people on your list who you can trust and who will be there to listen, support and encourage you. This may include spiritual support, community support or anything that helps you stay balanced and gives you strength.

Chapter 7

Approval

Embracing and Celebrating
a New Beginning

*"The secret of change is to focus all our energy
not on fighting the old but building the new."*

- Socrates

Choosing to Thrive

Human beings, in general, are resilient. We
bounce back after all types of loss, devastation
and regret. Hopefully, we use these times to push
through, find meaning and live the lessons learned
from the experience. The alternative is to be resentful,
bitter and broken. Resentments hold us back. They get
in the way of all we do and prevent us from having a
good life. We need to let go. In this case, letting go
means we are no longer willing to hold on to attitudes
and feelings that block spontaneity and love between
you and your child. Sometimes we let go because we
realize we are not willing to let a situation control our
happiness. Sometimes we let go because we realize
the pain of a circumstance stops hurting if I accept it.

Fortunately, we get to choose whether we want to survive in life or thrive.

Freedom from a former way of life takes time. With approval, you are letting go of struggle to hold on to the past as it was. You realize its time to put back the pieces and reinvest in yourself, your relationship to your child, to life. You know you can be happy and continue with purpose and passion.

Both acceptance and approval are positive responses. One can accept something and not approve of it. Acceptance means that you don't have to like something, but you agree to go along with it. Approval is going beyond acceptance. This is where you really get comfortable with your life, your child's transition, and know that it's not only permanent but also positive. You feel genuinely confident, open and positive to the gifts that you know will come as a result.

Some parents report there are no words to describe the warm feeling they feel each time they see their children happy as a result of their transition. You may have witnessed their journey from being sad and depressed, to having an unmistakable new zest for life. Your child may beam with enthusiasm and excitement about their appearance, career, friends, their future, and their relationship with you. You can appreciate that you may have been a significant part of their progress by being there with support. You can be proud of yourself for your ability to parent with love and to have allowed yourself to grow in your own transition.

Choosing Peace

"Peace isn't something you ultimately receive when you slow down the pace of your life. It isn't about merely choosing tranquil thoughts when you're feeling frayed and anxious. Peace is what you're capable of being and bringing to every encounter and events in the waking moments of your life. Suspend your ego and allow the higher, more spiritually based energies to weigh in toward your becoming more balanced."

Wayne Dyer - Being in Balance

At this stage, we get validity from our internal self. We learn that if we bend, we can remain whole. Approval gives you peace of mind, calmness, and a positive feeling about the future. Being peaceful allows us to be more productive and have a more balanced life. With peace we have a greater strength to use our coping skills and deal more confidently with whatever the future brings.

You deserve to have a good life. This includes learning new behaviors from time to time. Life is a good teacher. Sometimes we even come to a place where it all works out, where both you and your child can thrive. You can be grateful for all you have been through and find after all that, you can still sing the words to the song in your heart. We can always heal and go forward. With your love and support, the best may be yet to come.

Gifts of Approval

1) You get to be proud of yourself for all you are and all you've experienced. You appreciate that you are committed to your own transformation and emotional strength.

2) You realize that a relationship with your child is more important than gender. You understand that love goes beyond gender.

3) You know that you have made the world a better place by being empathetic and having compassion for yourself, your child and for all who get judged out of ignorance. You get to encourage, inspire and spread the truth, love and facts about gender diversity.

4) You trust that things happen at the right place, at the right time. You can soar to newer and

higher levels of awareness to create a new world of your own.

5) You have developed a deeper level of self-esteem, confidence, patience, strength, appreciation and love.

6) You get to embrace your choice to love and appreciate your role as a parent, to appreciate your child for living a life as they are, and to continue to create and cherish your relationship with your child.

7) You might find yourself wanting to share your knowledge and experience by volunteering in the gender community and taking an active stand against discrimination.

What to Say to Your Child

"I'm so lucky to have you as my child!"

"You'll always be my child and I will always love you."

"You will always be special to me."

"I love being a parent but I especially love being *your* parent."

To Yourself

"I love being the strong, competent and loving parent that I am."

"I am confident and trust myself to cope well and be kind to myself with any situation life brings me."

"I know the best gift I can give to others is to take care of myself."

Be proud of all you do and have done. You are stronger for all your experiences. Notice how things get easier to deal with. Appreciate yourself and the support you have given and received.

Trust yourself as a loving parent. Continue to create and look forward to a positive, loving and happy future for you and your child.

Glossary

<u>Androgynous</u> – When someone's presentation includes both masculine and feminine elements.

<u>Biological Sex</u> – The sex one is assigned at birth based on the appearance of the baby's genitals.

<u>Bisexual</u> – When an individual feels sexual attraction towards males and females.

<u>Cis or Cisgender</u> – A term used for people whose gender identity matches the sex they were assigned at birth.

<u>Male-to-Female</u> (MTF) – When a biological male from birth, changes his gender identity, gender expression and sometimes physical sex, to match that of his female gender. (To then be referred to as she, her and hers.)

<u>Female-to-Male</u> (FTM) – When a biological female at birth changes her gender identity, gender expression and sometimes physical sex, to

match that of her male gender. (To then be referred to as he, him and his.)

Pansexual – When an individual, feels love and sexual attraction towards others without placing importance on the partner's sex or gender.

Gender Dysphoria – Psychological term describing the feelings of pain, anguish, and anxiety when gender identity and physical sex do not match.

Gender Identity – One's internal sense of being male or female.

Gender Expression – The way in which a person expresses their gender, typically through their appearance, dress or behavior.

Gender Queer – A person who does not subscribe to conventional gender distinctions but identifies with neither, both, or a combination of male and female genders.

Gender Fluid – Someone who feels their gender identity is not fixed. It is a gender identity which can vary over time. A gender-fluid person may at any time identify as male, female, or any other non-binary identity. A gender-fluid identity can be a dynamic mix of male and female or be an identity that fluctuates between the two.

Gender Variant – Gender variant or gender non-conformity is behavior or gender expression by an individual that does not match masculine or feminine norms.

Intersex – Those born with ambiguous genitalia

Transgender – People who have a gender identity that is different from their biological/anatomical sex.

Transsexual – An outdated word for someone who is transgender.

Sexual Identity – One's sexual orientation that identifies who one is attracted to sexually.

Cross-Dresser – Person who enjoys wearing clothes identified with the opposite gender on a temporary basis.

Transition – This term is primarily used to refer to the social or medical transition process a transgender person undergoes when becoming more aligned with their true gender.

<u>Social Transition</u> – The time when a transgender
person begins presenting in public according
to his or her gender identity rather than
according to his or her biological sex. For
example, changing outward appearance.
(hair, clothing), making a name change,
telling others about your gender identity,
asking others to use pronouns that match
their true gender identity.

<u>Medical Transition</u> – When transgender people use
medical interventions and treatments, so
their bodies and sex characteristics better
match their gender Identity. For example,
using hormones or having surgery.